Berlitz ®

Rome

- A ☞ in the text denotes a highly recommended sight
- A complete A–Z of practical information starts on p.102
- Extensive mapping on cover flaps

Berlitz Publishing Company, Inc.

Princeton   Mexico City   Dublin   Eschborn   Singapore

Text: Jason Best
Editors: Nicola Gadsby, Sarah Hudson
Photography: Jon Davison, Jason Best
Layout: Media Content Marketing, Inc.
Cartography: ⊕ Falk-Verlag, Munich

Thanks to the staff of the Rome tourist board, Amanda Cruise and
Samantha Velluti.

*Found an error we should know about? Our editor would be happy
to hear from you, and a postcard would do. Although we make every
effort to ensure the accuracy of all the information in this book,
changes do occur.*

ISBN 2-8315-6370-4
Revised 1998 – First Printing March 1998

Printed in Switzerland by Weber SA, Bienne
019/803 REV

CONTENTS

ROME

ROME AND THE ROMANS

In the 27 centuries of its existence, Rome has seen empires rise and fall, popes and caesars come and go, and artistic movements flourish and fade. Throughout all the different eras, however, there has been one strong thread of continuity: the Eternal City has always been changing.

Rome certainly doesn't stand still today. As a modern European capital, it can't afford to rest on its laurels. Rome must play the part of an up-to-date political and business city while simultaneously attempting to preserve its enormous cultural inheritance.

The wealth of Rome's patrimony makes most other cities look like paupers. For a start, there are its great ancient remains: the Pantheon, still inspiring awe after almost 2,000 years; the terrible majesty of the Colosseum; the poignant ruins of the Roman Forum. Then there is the cool beauty of the early Christian basilicas and the heritage of medieval Rome, complete with all its glorious mosaics and tranquil cloisters. The Renaissance is reflected in elegant churches, graceful palaces, and the renowned genius of painters Raphael and Michelangelo. Finally, as if that wasn't enough, the Baroque era offers dynamic architecture, theatrical piazzas, and flamboyant fountains.

Visitors will quite likely be bowled over by this panoply of treasures, but today's Romans take them in their stride. They're accustomed to conducting their lives against this awesome backdrop, drinking tap water from an aqueduct which was probably constructed by a Roman consul and restored by a Renaissance pope.

Perhaps Romans take Rome too much for granted. It's refreshing that the city is not treated as an open-air museum, but less cheering that many museums and other treasures re-

7

main closed for years on end while bureaucrats wrangle over renovation costs and staffing levels. Medieval Romans burned marble statues to obtain lime; modern Romans' love affair with the internal-combustion engine does almost as much damage today. During the last few decades, exhaust fumes and traffic vibrations have had a catastrophic impact on monuments.

Some things are improving, however. Traffic has been banned from large areas of the historic centre, church façades have been given face-lifts, and scaffolding has been removed from ancient columns and triumphal arches.

Santa Francesca Romana church sits between the Forum and the Colosseum.

Today the magnificent equestrian bronze statue of Emperor Marcus Aurelius, which spent the 1980s undergoing restoration, is now firmly back on the Campidoglio, although it's behind protective glass in the Capitoline museums. In addition, billions of lire are now being spent on *Roma Capitale*, a massive programme of public works designed to enhance the status of the city.

Progress is evident but slow. The ancient Romans rushed out to conquer an empire and to make their city the *caput mundi* — "capital of the world." Their descendants

Piazza San Pietro (St. Peter's Square) — Bernini's greatest creation. On Sundays some 300,000 people flood the plaza.

have not been quite as quick off the mark. Since becoming the capital of the newly united Italy in 1870, Rome, as the nation's seat of government, has had a record somewhat marked by inefficiency and inertia. Despite the pressures of modern life, the hurtling traffic and bustling activity in markets and on the streets, the pace of life in Rome is really rather leisurely. Geographically as well as psychologically, the city is closer to the laid-back south than to the go-ahead north of Italy.

L'orario Americano, as the Italians call the 9-to-5 working day, has begun to gain ground in recent years, especially in the small-services sector and within large industries, although many small shops and businesses still close between 1:00 P.M. and 2:00 P.M., and between 3:00 P.M. and 4:00 P.M.; markets close down at 2:00 P.M. Many of those whose official working day finishes at 2:00 P.M. (in particular, State employees) go off to the undeclared second jobs that make Italy's black economy the biggest in Europe.

> **Every worker has the legal right to 20 paid vacation days during the summer and one week during the winter.**

Sidewalk cafés are an excellent place to soak up the atmosphere of Rome. This one is on the Piazza Navona.

Visitors should not fret over whether or not to follow the famous maxim of "When in Rome...." The rhythms of the Roman day will oblige you to do as the Romans do anyway. For instance, you'll soon discover that there's no point trying to toil round the sights in the afternoon heat, since most of the museums and churches will not be open. Rather, this is the time to join the natives and seek the shade of palms and pines in one of Rome's parks, formerly the exclusive preserve of cardinals and princes and now open to everyone.

Alternatively, you could sit soaking up the atmosphere in a tranquil piazza, admiring the play of sunlight on russet and ochre façades, listening to the water music of the continually splashing fountains, and enjoying one of the refreshing drinks the Romans do so well: perhaps a cool *spremuta d'arancio* made from freshly squeezed blood oranges, or a creamy *frullato* fruit shake.

When the city reawakens in the cool of the evening, join the Romans for their leisurely pre-dinner stroll, the *passeggiata*. This is the moment for greeting friends, exchanging news and, most importantly, checking out what everyone is wearing. You can be sure of one thing: many Romans youx see will be dressed up to the nines.

The streets begin to thin out after 8:00 P.M., and this is your cue to find somewhere to go and eat. Remember that the finest Roman cuisine is based on the cooking of the poor; so your most memorable meal may well be found in a cosy restaurant in the old Jewish ghetto or a traditional *trattoria* in the working-class district of Trastevere, rather than in a smarter establishment with a swankier address.

Whichever way you decide to spend your stay in Rome, there will always be pleasant surprises in store. Don't feel you have to plan every step in advance; instead, copy the young English aristocrat who came to Rome on his Grand Tour in 1780 and decided to "straggle and wander about just as the spirit chooses."

Rome will always reward those who put their trust in serendipity.

In the Vatican, another Bernini masterpiece: colonnade of Piazza San Pietro.

A BRIEF HISTORY

Cherished legend claims that Rome was founded by Romulus, sired with twin brother Remus by Mars of a vestal virgin and abandoned on the Palatine Hill to be suckled by a she-wolf. Historians agree that the site and traditional founding date of 753 B.C. are just about right.

Archaeologists have further established that the site was occupied as early in history as the Bronze Age (c. 1500 B.C.) and that by the eighth century B.C. villages had sprung up on the Palatine and Aventine hills and soon after on the Esquiline and Quirinal ridges. All these proved favourable spots for new settlements, as they were easily defensible and lay close to the midstream Isola Tiberina, which facilitated fording of the river. After conquering their Sabine neighbours, the Romans merged the group of villages into a single city and surrounded it with a defensive wall, while the marshland below the Capitoline Hill was drained and became the Forum. Under the consecutive rule of seven kings, the last three of whom were Etruscan, Rome began to develop as a powerful force in central Italy.

The Republic

A revolt by Roman nobles in 510 B.C. overthrew the last Etruscan king and established a Republic which was to last for the next five centuries. At first the young Republic, under the leadership of two patrician consuls, was plagued by confrontations between patrician and plebeian factions. But the plebs put forward their own leaders, the tribunes, to protect their interests. Strengthened internally by the new governing structure, Rome began to expand its influence.

In 390 B.C., the Gauls besieged the city for seven long months, destroying everything but the citadel on the Capitoline Hill. When the Gauls left, the hardy citizens set

Bridge over the river Tiber—the heart of Rome's historic district is the area enclosed by the bend of the river.

about reconstructing, this time enclosing their city in a wall of huge tufa blocks. For over eight centuries, until the Barbarians came, no foreign invader was to breach those walls.

Rome now spread its control to all of Italy, consolidating its hold with six military roads fanning out from the city— Appia, Latina, Salaria, Flaminia, Aurelia, and Cassia. By 250 B.C. the city's population had grown to an impressive 100,000.

Victory over Carthage in the hundred years of Punic wars (264-146 B.C.) and conquests in Macedonia, Asia Minor,

When Appius Claudius the Censor opened it in 312 B.C., the Appian Way was the grandest road in the Western world.

Spain, and southern France extended Roman power in the Mediterranean. When Hannibal crossed the Alps and invaded Italy in the Second Punic War, large areas of the peninsula were devastated and peasants sought refuge in Rome, swelling the population still further.

The acquisition of largely unsought territories brought new social and economic problems to the Roman people. Unemployment, poor housing, and an inadequate public works programme provoked unrest within the city. Violent civil wars shook the Republic, which ultimately yielded to dictatorship. Proconsul Julius Caesar, who had achieved some fame by subduing Gaul and Britain, crossed the tiny

Rubicon River, which marked the boundary of his province, and marched boldly on Rome to seize power.

The Empire

Caesar's reforms, which bypassed the Senate in order to combat unemployment, ease the tax burden, and make other reforms, made dangerous enemies. His assassination on the Ides of March in 44 B.C. led to a bitter civil war and to the despotic rule of his adopted son Octavian, who, as Augustus, became the first emperor. Under Augustus, the *Pax Romana* (Roman peace) reigned supreme over the far-flung empire. To make Rome a worthy capital, he added fine public buildings in the form of baths, theatres, and temples, claiming he had "found Rome brick and left it marble." He also intro-

The Colosseum, where aristocrat and plebeian alike once came to witness bloodshed.

The Arco de Settimio Severo (Arch of Septimius Severus) depicts his military triumphs.

duced public services, including the first fire brigade. This was also the Golden Age of Roman letters, distinguished by Horace, Ovid, Livy, and Virgil.

In the first centuries of the empire, tens of thousands of foreigners flooded into Rome, among them the first Christians, including St. Peter and St. Paul. As this "new religion" gained ground, the emperors tried to suppress it by means of persecution, but the steadfastness of the martyrs only increased its appeal.

Each of Augustus's successors contributed his own embellishments to Rome. After a disastrous fire ravaged the city in A.D. 64, Nero rebuilt it and provided himself with an ostentatious palace, the Domus Aurea (Golden House), on the Esquiline Hill. Hadrian reconstructed the Pantheon, raised a monumental mausoleum for himself (Castel Sant' Angelo), and retired to his magnificent estate, Villa Adriana at Tivoli.

In the late first and second centuries A.D. Rome reached the peak of its grandeur, with its population reaching over one million. Inherent flaws in the imperial system, however, be-gan to weaken the power of the emperors and led eventually to the total downfall of the empire.

After the death of Septimius Severus in A.D. 211, 25 emperors—all made and unmade by the armies—reigned in the short space of 74 years. Assassination was often the cause of the end of their reign. To add to the problems, fire and plague took their toll on the city's population, and in A.D. 283 the Forum was almost completely destroyed by fire—never to recover its former magnificence.

After a vision of the Cross appeared to him on a battlefield, the story goes, Emperor Constantine converted to Christianity. He ensured the religion was tolerated by an edict passed in A.D. 313, and he built the first churches and basilicas in Rome. But in A.D. 331 he dealt a fatal blow to the empire's unification when he moved the imperial seat to Byzantium (Constantinople). Many of the wealthy, as well as talented artists, joined him, a hemorrhage from which the old capital never recovered. Constantine's move effectively split the empire in two.

The Dark and Middle Ages

As the Western Empire went into decline, the Romans recruited Barbarians into the legions to help defend it against other outsiders. But the hired defenders soon joined the attackers, and the disenchanted and weary Roman populace failed to summon up the same enthusiasm to defend the city that they had shown in conquering an empire.

Wave after wave of dreaded Barbarians came to sack, rape, murder, and pillage—Alaric the Visigoth in A.D. 410, Attila the Hun, the Vandals, and the Ostrogoths. Finally the Barbarian chief Odoacer forced the last Roman emperor, Romulus Augustulus, to abdicate in 476. The Western Empire was at an end, although the Eastern Empire continued to prosper until 1453.

In the sixth century, Justinian reannexed Italy to the Byzantine Empire and codified Roman law as the state's legal system. But, as later Byzantine emperors lost interest, a new power arose out of the chaos in Rome: the Papacy. Pope

Leo I (440-461) had already asserted the Bishop of Rome as Primate of the Western Church and traced the succession back to St. Peter; and Pope Gregory the Great (A.D. 590-604) had shown statesmanship in warding off the Lombards, a Germanic tribe already established in the north of Italy. In the eighth century, citing a document, the *Donation of Constantine* (later found to be a forgery), the popes began to claim political authority over all of Italy.

Rome by this time had been reduced to a village, and its small population deserted the city when Barbarian invaders cut the imperial aqueducts. Seeking the powerful support of the Franks, Pope Leo III crowned their king, Charlemagne, ruler of the Holy Roman Empire in St. Peter's Basilica on Christmas Day A.D. 800. But the Pope had in turn to kneel in allegiance, and this exchange of spiritual blessing for military protection sowed the seeds of future conflict between popes and emperors.

Over the next 400 years, Italy saw invasions by Saracens and Magyars, Saxons and Normans (who were to sack Rome in 1084), with papal Rome struggling along as only one of many feudal city-states on the now tormented peninsula. The papacy, and with it Rome, was controlled by various powerful families from the landed nobility. As the situation in Rome degenerated into chaos—deplored by Dante in his *Divine Comedy*—the popes moved to comfortable exile in Avignon in 1309, and remained under the protection of the French king until 1377. Rome was left to the brutal rule of the Orsini and Colonna families.

Rome was sacked yet again, in 1084, this time by the determined Normans.

The Renaissance

The popes, reestablished in Rome in 1377, harshly put down any resistance to their rule and remained dominant in the city

Historical Landmarks

Earliest Beginnings
753 bc	Legendary founding of Rome
510	Establishment of Republic
390	Gauls sack the city
264–146	Punic Wars against Carthage
49	Julius Caesar seizes power.
44	Caesar assassinated in Rome.

Empire
27 bc	Augustus becomes first Roman emperor.
c. 64 ad	Persecution of Christians begins.
312	Constantine turns Christian.
331	Imperial capital moved to Byzantium.

Dark and Middle Ages
410	Visigoths sack Rome.
440-461	Pope Leo I asserts papal authority.
476	End of Western Roman Empire
800	Pope crowns Charlemagne in St. Peter's.
1084	Normans sack Rome.
1309–77	Popes exiled to Avignon.

Renaissance and Counter-Reformation
1508–12	Michelangelo paints Sistine Chapel ceiling.
1527	Sack of Rome by Imperial troops
1798–1809	Napoleon's troops enter Rome and establish a Republic.
1814	Pope restored with Austrian rule.
1861	Italy unified.
1870	Rome becomes capital of Italy.

Modern Era
1915	Italy enters World War I.
1922	Mussolini begins Fascist regime.
1929	Lateran Treaty creates separate Vatican state.
1940	Italy joins Germany in World War II.
1944	Allies liberate Rome.
1946	Monarchy abolished in favour of a Republic.

The dome of St. Peter's Basilica offers stunning views of the Vatican City and all of Rome.

for the next 400 years. During the 15th and 16th centuries, the papacy also became a notable patron of the Renaissance, that remarkable effusion of art and intellectual endeavour which gloriously transformed medieval Rome from a squalid, crumbling, and fever-ridden backwater to the foremost city of the Christian world.

It was Giorgio Vasari, facile artist and first-rate chronicler of this cultural explosion, who dubbed this movement a *rinascita,* or rebirth of the glories of Italy's Greco-Roman past.

The father of Rome's High Renaissance, Pope Julius II (1503–1513), was responsible for the new St. Peter's Basilica, and he also commissioned Michelangelo to paint the ceiling of the Sistine Chapel and Raphael to decorate the Stanze. Donato Bramante, the architect, got the nickname *maestro ruinante* because of the countless ancient monuments he had dismantled for the Pope's megalomaniacal building plans. With the treasures uncovered during this process, Julius founded the Vatican's magnificent collection of ancient sculpture.

The exuberant life of Renaissance Rome was brutally snuffed out in May 1527, however, by the arrival of mutinous troops of the invading German Emperor Charles V. It was to be the last—and worst—sack of the city.

Bernini's statue of David is one of many great works in the Galleria Borghese.

Counter-Reformation

Meanwhile the position of the papacy and doctrines of the Church of Rome were being challenged by Luther, Calvin, and other leaders of the Protestant Reformation.

The Counter-Reformation, formally proclaimed in 1563, reinforced the Holy Office's Inquisition to combat heresy and the Index to censor the arts. Italian Protestants fled and Jews in Rome were shut up in a ghetto.

Art proved a major instrument of Counter-Reformation propaganda. As the Church regained ground, it replaced the pagan influences of classicism with a more triumphant image, epitomized by Bernini's grand Baroque altar canopy in St. Peter's.

In the 18th century, Spain's authority over many of Italy's states passed to the Hapsburgs of Austria, who were determined to curb papal power in Rome. The papacy lost prestige with the enforced dissolution of the Jesuits, suffered a crippling loss of revenue from Hapsburg church reforms, and finally sank to its lowest ebb.

In 1798 Napoleon's troops entered Rome, later seized the Papal States, and proclaimed a Republic. They treated Pius VI with contempt and carried him off to be a virtual prisoner in France. His successor, Pius VII, was forced to proclaim Napoleon as emperor and for his pains was also made prisoner, returning to Rome only after Napoleon was defeated in 1814.

During the French occupation, however, a national self-awareness began to develop among Italians to challenge the reestablishment of Austrian rule. Many people looked to Pope Pius IX to lead this nationalist movement, but he feared the spread of liberalism and held back. In 1848, when a Republic was set up in Rome by Giuseppe Mazzini in the name of Italian nationalism, the Pope fled. He returned only in the following year, after the Republic had been crushed by the French army.

National unity for Italy was achieved in 1860 through the shrewd diplomacy of Cavour, the Prime Minister, the heroics of guerrilla general, Giuseppe Garibaldi, and the leadership of King Vittorio Emanuele of Piedmont. Rome was captured by the nationalists in 1870 and became capital of Italy in the following year. Pope Pius IX retreated to the Vatican, a "prisoner of the monarchy."

The Modern Era

In World War I Italy was on the winning side against Austria and Germany. But, after the peace conference of 1919, general disarray on the political scene led to an economic crisis, with stagnant productivity, bank closures, and rising unemployment. Threatened by the Fascists' March on Rome in 1922, King Vittorio Emanuele III meekly invited the Fascist leader, Benito Mussolini (Il Duce), to form a government.

Once firmly established in power, Mussolini made peace with the Pope by the Lateran Treaty of 1929, which created a separate Vatican state and perpetuated Catholicism as the national religion of Italy. In 1940 Mussolini plunged Italy into the Second World War on the side of the Germans. Rome was declared an open city to spare it from bombing and was liberated in 1944 with its treasures intact.

The initial post-war period was a time of hardship, but the 1950s saw Rome enjoying the fruits of Italy's "economic miracle." Jet-setting celebrities made the city their playground in the 1960s, finding *la dolce vita* in the nightspots of the Via Veneto. Meanwhile, Rome's population was soaring, as poor immigrants from Italy's south flocked into the city in search of work. Speculative developers threw up suburbs of shoddy blocks of flats on the urban periphery.

The city weathered a storm of left- and right-wing political terrorism when the 1970s became Italy's *anni di piombo* ("years of lead"). The darkest hour came in 1978 when the Red Brigades kidnapped and murdered the Democratic Prime Minister, Aldo Moro.

As Rome's ancient monuments are being scrubbed clean, a series of corruption scandals has revealed the dirty hands of the capital's politicians. In the hope of stability to come, Romans meanwhile have to get on with their daily lives, coping with the present, preparing for the future, and preserving the past.

WHERE TO GO

Visitors to Rome soon discover that remnants of the diverse eras which have influenced the city are often interwoven: a pagan mausoleum is also a papal fortress, a medieval church has a Baroque façade, and a Renaissance palace overlooks a modern traffic junction. It doesn't matter whether you've come to Rome for the grandeur of the ancient remains, the revered pilgrimage sites of the Catholic Church, or the inspired works of Michelangelo, Raphael, and Bernini —you'll end up seeing aspects of them all anyway.

Although the municipality of Rome sprawls over a huge area, the principal sights are packed into a comparatively small

In a city built on seven hills, you're never likely to be far from a splendid panoramic view.

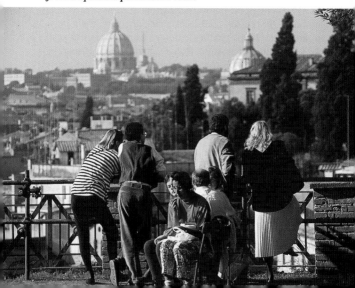

zone. The best way of getting about is on foot. Much of the historic centre has been closed to traffic, and driving elsewhere in the city can be hazardous for the uninitiated. Drivers are advised to leave their cars in a garage for the duration of their stay. Rome's public transport is often extremely crowded, but it will usually get you near enough to your destination. For the purpose of this guide we have grouped together places which can be most conveniently visited on the same walking tour.

Before you make a special trip to a museum or monument, it is best to check the current opening hours with the Tourist Office (see page 126) or your hotel, or look in the local newspapers (see page 117).

THE CENTRO STORICO

The heart of Rome's historic centre is the area enclosed by the bend of the River Tiber. Here, on what was once the Campus Martius, the "Field of Mars" where Roman soldiers exercised, you will find vestiges of Rome's many different eras: the remains of ancient temples, a maze of medieval streets, graceful Renaissance palaces, and ornate Baroque churches, sublime piazzas, and spectacular

> Underground fare in Rome is the same irrespective of the distance you travel.

fountains. But the city centre is up-to-date too — in amongst the monuments are the shops, hotels, and businesses of modern Rome.

Around Piazza Venezia

Piazza Venezia is the most convenient place to begin an exploration of Rome's Centro Storico. The hub of the capital's main traffic arteries, this is not really a piazza in which to linger, but it is on several major bus routes and in close proximity to a number of interesting sites.

The Essentials

For those making a brief visit to Rome, here are the very highest of the highlights:

ROMAN FORUM

CAMPIDOGLIO

COLOSSEUM

ST. PETER'S BASILICA

VATICAN MUSEUMS

SPANISH STEPS

TREVI FOUNTAIN

PIAZZA NAVONA

PANTHEON

An added advantage, as far as orientation is concerned, is the presence of the massive **il Vittoriano** (Vittorio Emanuele Monument), a landmark visible from all over the city. Romans wish the dazzling white edifice were not quite so conspicuous, and heap upon it such derisive nicknames as "Rome's False Teeth" and the "Wedding Cake." Built from 1885 to 1911 to celebrate the unification of Italy and dedicated to the new nation's first king, the Vittorio contains the tomb of Italy's Unknown Soldier of World War I.

A much more impressive work of architecture stands on the west side of the piazza: the **Palazzo Venezia**, the first great Renaissance palace in Rome. It was built for Cardinal Pietro Barbo, later Pope Paul II, supposedly so that he could watch the horse races along the Corso in comfort. Later it became the embassy of the Venetian Republic to the Holy See, and in this century served as Mussolini's official headquarters. His desk stood at the far corner of the vast Sala del Mappamondo, so positioned to intimidate visitors who had to approach across the full length of the marble floor. From the small balcony over the central door in the façade, *Il Duce* harangued his followers amassed in the square below. The palace now contains a museum of mediaeval and Renaissance furniture, arms, tapestries, ceramics, and sculpture.

The Capitoline Hill

Two flights of steps lead up behind the Vittorio Emanuele Monument. The more graceful and gradual, known as La Cordonata, takes you up between colossal statues of the heavenly twins, Castor and Pollux, to the tranquil elegance of the **Campidoglio**, on top of the Capitoline Hill.

This was once the Capitol, where the Temple of Jupiter Optimus Maximus Capitolinus stood, the most sacred site of all in ancient Rome. Today the Campidoglio is the site of a glorious Renaissance square, designed by Michelangelo, on the command of Pope Paul III, for the reception of the Holy Roman Emperor Charles V. Michelangelo also remodelled the existing **Palazzo Senatorio**, Rome's town hall down

---

The First Capitol Hill

To the Romans, the Capitol was both citadel and sanctuary, the symbolic centre of government, where the consuls took their oath and the Republic's coinage was minted. Its name, now applied to many governments across the world (notably Congress in Washington), originated in a legend that the skull of a mythical hero was unearthed here during excavations for the Temple of Juno. Augurs interpreted this as a sign that Rome would one day be head (*caput*) of the world.

When the Gauls sacked Rome in 390 B.C., the Capitol was saved by the timely cackling of the sanctuary's sacred geese, warning that attackers were scaling the rocks.

Later, victorious caesars ended their triumphal processions here. They rode up from the Forum in chariots drawn by white steeds to pay homage at the magnificent gilded Temple of Jupiter, which dominated the southern tip of the Capitoline.

In the Middle Ages, the collapsed temples were pillaged and the hill was abandoned to goats until, in the 16th century, Pope Paul III commissioned Michelangelo to give it new glory.

through the ages, and planned the two palaces which flank it, the Palazzo dei Conservatori and the Palazzo Nuovo, although other architects completed them after his death.

As a centrepiece for the piazza, Michelangelo placed the magnificent gilded **statue of Marcus Aurelius** in the square. The oldest equestrian bronze in the world, dating back to the second century A.D., it had survived because the pagan emperor had been mistaken for the Christian Constantine. According to legend, it was so lifelike that Michelangelo commanded it to walk. Having recently emerged from a long period of restoration, the statue is now displayed, behind glass, in the Palazzo Nuovo.

The **Capitoline Museums**, in the palaces of the Campidoglio, have extensive collections of magnificent sculpture excavated from ancient Rome. The **Palazzo Nuovo** contains row upon row of portrait busts of Roman emperors (a good introduction to Classical Rome—see page 44), although its highlights are the poignant statue of the *Dying Gaul*, the sensual *Capitoline Venus*, a Roman copy of a Greek original dating from the second century B.C., and the *Marble Faun*, which gave its name to Hawthorne's romance. In the courtyard of the **Palazzo dei Conservatori** are a giant marble head, hand, and foot: fragments from a colossal statue of Emperor Constantine. The palace is also home to the famous **Capitoline She-Wolf** depicted suckling the infants Romulus and Remus. This Etruscan bronze dating from the fifth century B.C. has become the symbol of Rome. (Pollaiuolo embellished the statue somewhat.) In the nearby **Pinacoteca Capitolina** (Capitoline Picture Gallery) are many fine works by Caravaggio, Bellini, Velázquez, Rubens, and Titian.

Alongside the Palazzo Senatorio a cobbled road opens out on to a terrace, giving you the first glimpse of the ruins of the Roman Forum (page 44), stretching from the Arch of Septimius Severus to the Arch of Titus, with the Colosseum

The Etruscan bronze she-wolf, depicted suckling the infants Romulus and Remus, has become the symbol of Rome.

beyond. On your right is the infamous Tarpeian Rock, from which the Romans hurled traitors to their deaths.

The steeper flight of steps up the Campidoglio climbs to the austere church of **Santa Maria in Aracoeli**, on the site of the great temple of Juno Moneta, where the Tiburtine Sibyl announced the coming of Christ to Augustus. The 13th-century church harbours the curious and much-revered Bambino, kept in a separate little chapel. Some Romans like to attribute miraculous healing powers to this statue of the infant Jesus, and stacks of unopened letters from all over the world addressed to Il Bambino surround the jewel-bedecked figure. At Christmas the statue becomes the centre-piece of the manger scene, before which young children recite short poems and speeches.

The Corso

The mile-long main street of central Rome runs in a straight line from Piazza Venezia to Piazza del Popolo. Known in an-cient times as the *Via Lata*, the Corso derives its modern name from the carnival races, or *corse,* that were first held here in the 15th century under the spectacle-loving Venetian Pope Paul II. Of all the races, the most thrilling was the *Corsa dei Barberi*, in which riderless Barbary horses, sent into a frenzy by saddles spiked with nails, charged pell-mell along the narrow thoroughfare to be halted at last by a large white sheet hung across the street. Today the Corso is lined with palaces and churches, and crowded with shops and shoppers. Probably the busiest of Rome's streets, it is liveliest during the hour of the evening stroll or *passeggiata* (see page 11).

In the **Piazza Colonna**, the **column of Marcus Aurelius**, decorated with spiralling reliefs of the emperor's military triumphs, rises in front of the Italian prime minister's offices in the Chigi Palace. The statue of the soldier-emperor, which originally stood on top of the column, was replaced in 1589 by a statue of St. Paul.

On the **Piazza Montecitorio** next door, which is dominated by an Egyptian obelisk dating from the sixth century B.C., stands the **Camera dei Deputati** (Chamber of Deputies), Italy's legislative lower house, designed by Bernini as a palace for the Ludovisi family.

If you turn off the Corso to the banks of the River Tiber, you can visit the **Ara Pacis Augustae**, a fascinating monument housed in a glass-sided building. When fragments of this "Altar of Peace," commissioned to celebrate Augustus's victorious campaigns in Gaul and Spain, first came to light in 1568, they were dispersed among several European museums. The pieces were returned to Rome when reconstruction began earlier this century. Along the friezes you can make out Augustus himself, with his wife Livia and daughter Julia, friend Agrippa, and a host of priests, nobles, and dignitaries. Alongside the Altar, the great mound encircled by cypresses is the **Mausoleum of Augustus**, repository of the ashes of the caesars until Hadrian built his own mausoleum (now the

Artists Galore

A host of artists and architects contributed to Rome's splendour. Here are some of the most influential.

BERNINI, GIAN LORENZO (1598–1680). As painter, sculptor, and architect, the foremost exponent of Baroque art. St. Peter's Square, Fountain of the Four Rivers, Palazzo Barberini, Galleria Borghese, S. Maria della Vittoria.

BORROMINI, FRANCESCO (1599–1667). Baroque architect, assistant to and later great rival of Bernini. Sant'Agnese in Agone, Palazzo Barberini.

BRAMANTE, DONATO (1444–1514). Architect and painter from Urbino. Foremost architect of High Renaissance. St. Peter's, Belvedere Courtyard in the Vatican.

CAMBIO, ARNOLFO DI (c. 1245–1302). Gothic architect and sculptor from Pisa. Statue of St. Peter in St. Peter's Basilica, tabernacle in St. Paul's.

CANOVA, ANTONIO (1757–1822). Neo-classical sculptor. Statue of Napoleon's sister Pauline in the Borghese Gallery.

CARAVAGGIO, MICHELANGELO MERISI DA (1571–1610). Revolutionized art in the early 17th century. Paintings in Santa Maria del Popolo, San Luigi dei Francesi, Palazzo Barberini, S. Agostino, Quadreria della Galleria Borghese a S. Michele a Ripa.

MADERNO, CARLO (1556–1629). Architect from northern Italy. Façade of St. Peter's, papal palace at Castel Gandolfo.

MICHELANGELO BUONARROTI (1475–1564). Florentine painter, sculptor, and architect, one of the most influential men in the history of art. Dome of St. Peter's Basilica, Sistine Chapel ceiling, *Moses* in San Pietro in Vincoli, Campidoglio.

PINTURICCHIO, BERNARDINO (c. 1454–1513). Frescoes in Sistine Chapel, Borgia Apartments, and Santa Maria del Popolo.

RAPHAEL (RAFFAELLO SANZIO) (1483–1520). Painter and architect of High Renaissance. Stanze in Vatican, Chigi Chapel in Santa Maria del Popolo, *La Fornarina* in Palazzo Barberini.

The Villa Borghese contains the Piazza di Siena pictured here, as well as a zoo.

Castel Sant'Angelo, see page 54) on the other side of the Tiber.

At its northern end, the Corso culminates in the graceful oval shape of the **Piazza del Popolo**, a truly exemplary piece of open-air urban theatre designed in 1818 by Giuseppe Valadier, former architect to Napoleon. The central obelisk, dating back to the Egypt of Ramses II (13th century B.C.), was brought to Rome by Augustus and erected in the Circus Maximus. Pope Sixtus V had it moved here in 1589.

The square takes its name from the Renaissance church of **Santa Maria del Popolo**, built on the site of Nero's tomb to exorcize his ghost, reputed to haunt the area. Its Baroque interior is famous for its works of art. They include a superb fresco of the *Nativity* by Pinturicchio, and Raphael's Chigi Chapel, built as a mausoleum for the family of the wealthy Sienese banker and patron of the arts, Agostino Chigi. This chapel houses two fine sculptures by Bernini: *Habakkuk* and *Daniel and the Lion*. In the Cerasi Chapel are two powerful works by Caravaggio, the *Conversion of St. Paul* and *Crucifixion of St. Peter*, notable for the dramatic use of light and shade and the skillful foreshortening of the figures.

Next to the church, the arched 16th-century **Porta del Popolo** marks the gateway to ancient Rome at the end of the Via Flaminia, which led from Rimini on the Adriatic Coast. Pilgrims arriving in Rome by the gate were greeted by the two imposing Baroque churches of Santa Maria dei Miracoli and Santa Maria de Montesanto, both guarding the northern entrance to the Corso.

To the east above the piazza, and reached by a monumental complex of terraces, the **Pincio** gardens offer a magical view of the city, especially at sunset, when the rooftops are tinged with purple and gold. Also the work of Valadier, the gardens occupy the site of the first-century B.C. villa of Lucullus. This provincial governor returned enriched by the spoils of Asia and impressed his contemporaries by his extravagant lifestyle. The gardens stretch on into the less formal park of the **Villa Borghese**, once the estate of Cardinal Scipione Borghese, the nephew of Pope Paul V. The extensive grounds contain the recently renovated Galleria Borghese (see page 72), housed in the cardinal's former summer palace, and a zoo to the north.

Lined with pine trees and open-air cafés, the Pincio promenade takes you past the **Villa Medici**, built in 1544 and bought by Napoleon as a home for the French National Academy. Today the villa is host to young French artists visiting Rome on scholarships.

Around the Piazza di Spagna

Now the city's most fashionable shopping district, the area around the **Piazza di Spagna** has been attracting foreigners for centuries. Aristocratic travellers on the Grand Tour came here, as did many of the most celebrated artists of the Romantic era, among them Keats (see below), Byron, Balzac, Wagner, and Liszt.

The area continues to attract a cosmopolitan crowd. Well-heeled visitors come for the elegant and exclusive high-fashion shops along the Via Condotti and its neighbouring streets. Meanwhile, the more casually shod linger on the glorious **Scalinata della Trinità dei Monti** (the Spanish Steps), the city's most popular rendezvous for young Romans and foreigners alike. The steps ascend in three majestic tiers to the 16th-century church of **Trinità dei Monti**, which, with twin belfries and a graceful Baroque façade, is one of Rome's most distinctive landmarks. Pink azaleas adorn the steps in spring, and in summer they become the catwalk for an open-air fashion show at which top international designers present new evening-wear collections.

> An **EDICOLA** is an outdoor kiosk that sells newspapers and often tickets for public transportation.

At the foot of the steps lies the **Fontana di Barcaccia**, a marble fountain in the shape of a leaking boat. The design, variously attributed to Pietro Bernini or his more famous son, Gianlorenzo, is an ingenious solution to the problem of low pressure in the Acqua Vergine, the aqueduct that supplies the fountain with water.

The poet John Keats died in 1821 in a small room overlooking the steps. His house, 26 Piazza di Spagna, has since been preserved as the **Keats-Shelley Memorial** and museum. On the other side of the steps, at number 23, the quintessentially English **Babington's Tea Rooms** is a pleasant oasis of Anglo-Saxon calm and gentility that has been serving tea and scones since the 1890s, when it was opened by a Miss Babington and her friend Miss Cargill.

An even more venerable establishment is found on nearby Via Condotti. **Caffè Greco** has been a favoured haunt of writers and artists for over two centuries, and the autographed portraits, busts, and statues decorating the café attest to its distinguished clientèle, among them Casanova,

The Fontana dei Fiumi symbolizes the great rivers of the Americas, Europe, Asia, and Africa.

Goethe, Baudelaire, Buffalo Bill, Gogol, and Hans Christian Andersen.

Approached through a maze of narrow alleyways, the **Fontana di Trevi** (Trevi Fountain) never fails to astonish. Nicola Salvi's Rococo extravaganza seems a giant stage set, out of all proportion to its tiny piazza. The 18th-century fountain is in fact a triumphal arch and palace façade (for the old Palazzo Poli) which frames mythic creatures in a riot of rocks and pools. The centrepiece is the massive figure of Neptune, who rides on a seashell drawn by two winged sea horses led by tritons. The rearing horse symbolizes the sea's turmoil, the calm steed its tranquillity. Marcello Mastroianni and Anita Ekberg frolicked memorably in the fountain's legendarily pure waters when they starred in Federico Fellini's film *La Dolce Vita*. The authorities frown on that sort of behaviour today, but you can throw a coin in over your shoulder to ensure a return to Rome.

Dominating the summit of the highest of the seven hills of ancient Rome is the Baroque **Palazzo del Quirinale**. This was the summer palace of the popes until the unification of Italy in 1870, when it became home of the new King of Italy. Since 1947 it has been the official residence of the President of the Republic. In the centre of the vast Piazza del Quirinale, magnificent **statues of Castor and Pollux** and their steeds, all Roman copies of Greek originals, stand beside an ancient obelisk. The piazza affords a splendid panoramic view over the whole city towards St. Peter's.

A Shocking Painter

Hot-tempered in life and a revolutionary in art, Michelangelo Merisi da Caravaggio single-handedly overturned the conventions of religious painting. His bold use of foreshortening and dramatic *chiaroscuro* have lost none of their force today, but it was his earthy realism that really shocked his contemporaries.

Caravaggio painted St. Matthew with peasant hands and a wrinkled brow for the church of San Luigi dei Francesi near the Piazza Navona and was accused of irreverence. Furthermore, he was rumoured to have used a prostitute as the model for the Virgin Mary in his painting of the *Madonna of Loreto*, which hangs in the nearby church of Sant'Agostino. We know from the court records of the day that the prostitute, who plied her trade in Piazza Navona, was the cause of a quarrel in which Caravaggio wounded a notary in the summer of 1605.

A year later, the painter was forced to flee Rome after killing a man in a brawl that started over a game of racquets. There followed spells in Naples, Malta, and Sicily and further scrapes with the authorities. He died of a fever in Port'Ercole in 1610, just as efforts were being made to gain him a pardon in Rome.

Lovers of the Baroque era will find much to delight them in this part of the city, which teems with masterpieces of sculpture and architecture by Bernini. Opposite the *manica lunga* or "long sleeve" of the Quirinal Palace you will find the small but perfectly formed church of **Sant'Andrea al Quirinale**, while in the nearby **Piazza Barberini** are two of the master's celebrated fountains: the **Fontana del Tritone**, which takes centre stage, and the **Fontana delle Api**, on its north side. Both fountains sport the bee symbol taken from the Barberini coat of arms of Pope Urban VIII, Bernini's patron.

The busy genius also had a hand in the architecture of the stately **Palazzo Barberini**, which now houses part of the Galleria Nazionale d'Arte Antica (see page 75).

A short distance away, but well worth the walk, is the church of **Santa Maria della Vittoria**, home to one of the supreme works of Baroque sculpture, Bernini's *Ecstasy of St. Theresa*. Based on a mystical vision experienced by Theresa of Avila, the statue shows the saint in the throes of a religious rapture that appears to be as much erotic as spiritual.

Around the Piazza Navona

The **Piazza Navona** has been a prime spot for Roman recreation since the time of Emperor Domitian, who laid out an athletics stadium, *Circus Agonalis*, on the site in A.D. 79, establishing the future square's oval shape.

Jousting tournaments took place here in the Middle Ages, and from the 17th-19th centuries it was the scene of spectacular water pageants in summer, when the fountains overflowed until the piazza was flooded. As bands played, the aristocracy drove through the water in their gilded coaches, to the delight of onlookers. Today the piazza remains a colourful and lively spot. Sit at a pavement table of one of the cafés and enjoy the spectacle supplied by artists, buskers, and caricaturists.

The Baroque centrepiece is Bernini's **Fontana dei Fiumi** (Fountain of the Four Rivers), which incorporates an ancient obelisk into a monumental allegory symbolizing the great rivers of the Americas (Río de la Plata), Europe (the Danube), Asia (the Ganges), and Africa (the Nile). Romans who delight in Bernini's scorn for his rivals suggest that the Nile god is covering his head rather than have to look at Borromini's church of Sant'Agnese in Agone, and that the river god of the Americas is poised to catch it in case it collapses. In truth, the fountain was completed some years before Borromini's splendid — and indeed structurally impeccable — façade and dome.

The **Pantheon**, in the Piazza della Rotonda, which always impresses visitors, is the best-preserved monument of ancient Rome. This "Temple of all the Gods" was saved for posterity when it was converted into a church in the seventh century. The original Pantheon, built on this site in 27 B.C. by Marcus Agrippa, was destroyed by fire. Emperor Hadrian then rebuilt it around A.D. 125, but modestly left his predecessor's name on the frieze above the portico, which is supported by 16 monolithic pink-and-grey granite columns. The bronze beams which once adorned the entrance were taken away by the Barberini Pope Urban VIII to make Bernini's canopy for the high altar in St. Peter's. His action prompted the saying: "Quod non fecerunt barbari, fecerunt Barberini" ("What the Barbarians didn't do, the Barberini did").

The Pantheon's true greatness is only fully appreciated once you step inside and look up into the magnificent coffered **dome**. Over 43 metres (141 feet) in diameter (exactly equal to its height), and even larger than the mighty cupola of St. Peter's, the dome represents an unparalleled feat of architecture and engineering. On fine days a shaft of sunlight

*Campo dei Fiori, the "field of flowers," is the
fitting location for this colourful stall.*

lights up the windowless vault through the circular hole
(*oculus*) in the dome (it also lets in the rain). The gods and
goddesses are long gone, replaced by the Renaissance tombs
of Raphael and the architect Baldassare Peruzzi, as well as
the modern kings Vittorio Emanuele II and Umberto I.

Around the Campo dei Fiori

The site of public executions during the 17th century, the
Campo dei Fiori is now a bustling fruit, vegetable, and
flower market. A reminder of the square's bloody past, however, is provided by the statue of philosopher Giordano
Bruno, who was burned at the stake here by the Inquisition
in 1600 for his heretical belief that the earth revolves around
the sun, and not vice versa as the Church proclaimed. An
even more famous death occurred at the nearby Piazza del

This neo-Babylonian synagogue is linked to a museum of Jewish history.

Biscione, or more precisely the restaurant Da Pancrazio, whose cellar holds the ruins of Pompey's theatre, where Julius Caesar was assassinated.

The great architects of the age worked on the **Palazzo Farnese**, Rome's finest Renaissance palace. Begun in 1514 by Antonio da Sangallo the Younger for Cardinal Alessandro Farnese (Pope Paul III), the project was passed on to Michelangelo, and it was finally completed in 1589 by Giacomo della Porta. The building cost so much that it put a great strain on the fortune Farnese had amassed while he was Treasurer of the Church. Since 1871 the palace has been home to the French Embassy. You need special permission to see the ceremonial dining room's mythological frescoes by Annibale Carracci. Facing Palazzo Farnese, on the left of the square, is Palazzo Spada, a beautiful example of Renaissance art which houses a museum and art gallery.

The narrow streets heading southeast of the Campo dei Fiori take you into the former **Jewish ghetto**, a lively and historic district peppered with restaurants serving the city's distinctive Roman/Jewish cuisine. A feature of Roman life for more than 2,000 years, Jews were forced into a ghetto in the 16th century by Pope Paul IV. The walls that confined the quarter were torn down in 1848, but a small Jewish community still lives around the Via del Portico d'Ottavia. The neo-Babylonian synagogue down by the river is linked to a museum of Jewish history.

One of the most charming fountains in Rome, the 16th-century **Fontana delle Tarturughe** (Turtle Fountain), can be found in Piazza Mattei. It depicts four boys perched on dolphins while lifting four turtles into a marble basin with gracefully outstretched arms.

The nearby **Portico d'Ottavia**, a crumbling arched façade more than 2,000 years old and dedicated to Augustus' sister, once enclosed temples to Jupiter and Juno. Beyond it extends the **Teatro di Marcello** (Theatre of Marcellus), begun by Augustus and the architectural model for the Colosseum.

The Ponte Fabricio, Rome's oldest bridge (62 B.C.), links the left bank to the **Isola Tiberina.** Three centuries before Christ the island was sacred to Aesculapius, god of healing, to whom a temple and hospital were dedicated. A hospital still stands here to this day, tended by the Brothers of St. John of God. A second bridge, Ponte Cestio, remodelled in the 19th century, leads over to the right bank of the river Tiber and Trastevere (see page 43).

The Aventine

Once revered as the "Sacred Mount" in ancient times, when it stood outside Rome's walls, the Aventine remains a quiet sanctuary above the clamour of the city. An aristocratic district in the Imperial era, the hill is still a favoured residential zone, with villas and apartments set in shady gardens of flowers and palms.

The Aventine is also the site of some of the earliest Christian churches, the most beautiful of which is the basilica of **Santa Sabina**. Here a classical harmony is given by the 24 white Corinthian columns lining the nave, while the beautiful carved cypress-wood doors in the portico contain one of the earliest depictions of the crucifixion in Christian art. The doors date back to the fifth century, as does the basilica itself. Through a window in the atrium you can see a descendant of an orange tree planted by St. Dominic in 1220. A few steps away stands the villa of the Cavalieri di Malta (Knights of Malta). Take a peep through the keyhole of the garden door for an unusual view of the dome of St. Peter's.

At the foot of the Aventine near the Tiber, the little church of **Santa Maria in Cosmedin** was given to Rome's Greek colony in the Middle Ages. Its Romanesque façade and simple interior provide stark contrast to the city's dominant Baroque grandeur. Test your honesty in the portico's fierce-looking **Bocca della Verità** (Mouth of Truth). The ancient marble face is said to bite off the fingers of anyone with his hand in the gaping mouth who tells a lie.

Across the road, two of the city's most charming and best-preserved temples stand on what was once part of the ancient cattle market. The one with fluted marble columns is erroneously known as the **Temple of Vesta**—probably dedicated to Hercules. Its rectangular neighbour, the **Temple of Fortune**, is a victim of the Classical scholars' equivalent of a typing error, as its presiding deity is believed to have been Portunus, god of harbours, rather than Fortuna. From the parapet of the Ponte Palatino, the mouth of the **Cloaca Maxima**, the great drain of ancient Rome, is visible at low tide. Begun by King Tarquin in around 600 B.C., the sewer is still in use today.

South of the Aventine near Porta San Paolo, dark cypresses shade the beautiful **Protestant Cemetery,** where Keats is buried (see page 34) and where Shelley's ashes are interred. Towering over the cemetery is Rome's only **pyramid**, incorporated into the city walls. A Roman colonial magistrate,

Caius Cestius, commissioned it for his tomb in 12 B.C. on his return from duty in Egypt.

Trastevere

Trastevere has been Rome's traditional working-class quarter "across the Tiber" (*Tevere*) since ancient times, and its inhabitants pride themselves on being the true Romans, a breed apart from the rest of the city. The word *Noiantri*, dialect for "we others," reflects the way they see themselves, and is also the name for their riverside July festival of music and fireworks.

Despite recent gentrification which has dotted the district with smart shops, tearooms, clubs, and restaurants, Trastevere still displays its lively atmosphere and idiosyncratic character, particularly in the narrow cobbled streets around the Piazza di Santa Maria, the heart of the quarter. The church of **Santa Maria in Trastevere** is reputedly the oldest in the city. Its foundation (on the spot where oil is said to have gushed to presage the birth of Christ) can be traced back to the third century, but the present structure dates from 1130-1143 and is the work of Pope Innocent II, himself a Trasteverino. The façade is decorated with a beautiful and mysterious 12th-century mosaic of the Virgin flanked by ten maidens bearing lamps.

Before entering the church of **Santa Cecilia in Trastevere**, pause in the courtyard to admire the russet Baroque façade and endearingly leaning Romanesque tower. Now regarded as the patron saint of music, St. Cecilia was martyred for her Christian faith in 230. Her chapel stands over the site of the *caldarium* (bathhouse) in which she was tortured by scalding. The sculptor Stefano Maderno was on hand when her tomb was excavated in 1599 and his beautiful statue shows how the body then appeared, miraculously undecomposed.

CLASSICAL ROME

The nucleus of classical Rome is around the Colosseum (see page 51), with the Forum to the northwest (see below) and the Baths of Caracalla (see page 52) to the south. Don't try to decipher each fragment of broken stone—not even archaeologists can do that. It's far better to soak up the romantic atmosphere while reflecting on the ruined majesty of this ancient civilization. Take care to avoid the midday sun in the shadeless Forum and finish your visit with a picnic and siesta on the Palatine.

The Roman Forum

With an exhilarating leap of the imagination, you can stand among the columns, porticoes, and arches of the *Foro Romano* and picture the hub of the great Imperial city, the first in Europe to house a million people.

Surrounded by the Palatine, Capitoline, and Esquiline hills and drained by the Cloaca Maxima, an underground channel (see page 42), the flat valley of the Forum developed as the civic, commercial, and religious centre of the growing city.

Under the emperors, it attained unprecedented splendour, with its white marble and the golden roofs of temples, law courts, and market halls glittering in the sun. After the Barbarian invasions, the area was abandoned. Subsequently fire, earthquakes, floods, and the plunder of Renaissance architects reduced the area to a muddy cow pasture, until the excavations of the 19th century once again brought many of the ancient edifices to light. Grass still grows between the cracked paving stones of the Via Sacra, poppies bloom in among the piles of toppled marble, and tangles of red roses are entwined in the brick columns, softening the harshness of the ruins.

Few ancient buildings can match the massive proportions of the Roman Forum's Basilica of Maxentius.

Portable sound-guides can be rented at the entrance (on the Via dei Fori Imperiali) or you can find your own way round the Forum. But before you embark on this, a sensible move is to make yourself comfortable on a chunk of fallen marble in the midst of the ruins and orient yourself, with the help of a detailed plan, so that you can trace the layout of the buildings and make sense of the apparent confusion.

Start your tour at the west end, just below the Campidoglio's Palazzo Senatorio (see page 27). Here you can see how the arches of the Roman record office (*Tabularium*) have been incorporated into the rear of the Renaissance palace. From here, look along the full length of the **Via Sacra** (Sacred Way), the route taken by victorious generals as they rode in triumphal procession to the foot of the Capitoline

Hill, followed by the legions' standards, massed ranks of prisoners, and carts piled high with the spoils of conquest.

Then, to counterbalance this image of the Romans as ruthless military conquerors, turn to the brick-built rectangular **Curia**, home of the Roman Senate, in the northwest corner of the Forum. Here you can gaze through the bronze doors (copies of the originals which are now in the church of St. John Lateran; see page 67) at the "venerable great-grandmother of all parliaments," where the senators, robed in simple togas, argued the affairs of Republic and Empire. It's worth noting that the tenets of Roman law, which underpins most Western legal systems, were first debated in this modest chamber.

Believed to mark the site of the very first assembly hall of the Roman elders, the Curia was constructed in its present form by Diocletian in A.D. 303. Its plain brick façade was once faced with marble. The church that covered it was dismantled in 1937 to reveal an ancient floor set with geometrical patterns in red and green marble, as well as the tiers on either side where the Roman senators sat, and the brick base of the golden statue of Victory at the rear. The Curia shelters two bas-reliefs, possibly from the Rostra (see below), outlining in marble the ancient buildings of the Forum.

In front of the Curia, a concrete shelter protects the underground site of the **Lapis Niger** (usually not on view), a black marble stone placed by Julius Caesar over the (presumed) grave of Romulus, the city's founder. Beside it is a stele engraved with the oldest Latin inscription ever found, dating back some six centuries before Christ; no one has completely deciphered it yet.

The triple **Arco de Settimio Severo** (Arch of Septimius Severus) dominates this end of the Forum. Its friezes depict the eastern military triumphs of the third-century emperor who later campaigned as far as Scotland and died in York. Nearby is the orators' platform, or **Rostra**, from which Mark

Antony stirred the crowds into a frenzy after Julius Caesar's assassination. Its name comes from the iron prows (*rostra*), which once adorned it, taken from enemy ships at the Battle of Antium in 338 B.C.

Two points have special significance: the *Umbilicus Urbis Romae*, which marks the traditional centre of Rome, and the *Miliarium Aureum* (Golden Milestone), which recorded in gold letters the distances in miles from Rome to the provinces of the empire.

Public meetings and ceremonies took place in the social forum in front of the Rostra, kept bare save for samples of three plants essential to Mediterranean prosperity: the vine, the olive, and the fig. Still prominent above this open space is the **Colonna di Foca** (Column of Phocas), built to honour the Byzantine emperor who presented the Pantheon to Pope Boniface IV.

Eight tall columns standing on a podium at the foot of the Capitol belong to the **Tempio di Saturno** (Temple of Saturn), one of the earliest temples in Rome. It doubled as both state treasury and centre of the December debauchery know as the Saturnalia, the pagan precursor of Christmas.

Of the **Basilica Julia**, once busy law courts, only the paving and some of the arches and travertine pillars survive. Even less remains of the Basilica Aemilia, on the opposite side of the Via Sacra, destroyed by the Goths in A.D. 410.

Three slender columns, the podium, and a portion of the entablature denote the **Tempio dei Dioscuri** (Temple of Castor and Pollux), built 484 B.C. It was dedicated to the twin sons of Jupiter (the Dioscuri) after they appeared on the battlefield at Lake Regillus to rally the Romans against the Latins and the Etruscans.

The altar of Julius Caesar is tucked away in a semicircular recess of the **Tempio di Cesare** (Temple of the Divine Julius). On 19 March in 44 B.C., the grieving crowds, following Caesar's funeral procession to his cremation in the Campus Martius, made an impromptu pyre of chairs and tables and burned his body in the Forum.

Pause for a pleasant idyll in the **Casa delle Vestali** (Hall of the Vestal Virgins), surrounded by graceful statues in the serene setting of a rose garden and old rectangular fountain basins, once more filled with water. In the circular white marble **Tempio di Vesta** (the Temple of Vesta), the sacred flame perpetuating the Roman state was tended by six Vestal Virgins who from childhood observed a 30-year vow of chastity under threat of being buried alive if they broke it. They were under the supervision of the high priest, the Pontifex Maximus (the popes have since appropriated this title), whose official residence was in the nearby Regia, of which only overgrown brick vestiges remain.

The imposing **Temple of Antoninus and Faustina,** farther along the Via Sacra, has survived because, like the Curia, it was converted into a church, acquiring a Baroque façade in 1602. In addition, few ancient buildings can match the massive proportions of the **Basilica of Maxentius**, completed by Constantine (whose name it also bears). Three giant vaults still stand.

The Via Sacra culminates in the **Arch of Titus**, built to commemorate the capture of Jerusalem in A.D. 70. Restored by Giuseppe Valadier in 1821, it shows in magnificent carved relief the triumphal procession of Titus bearing the spoils of the city, among them the Temple of Jerusalem's seven-branched golden candlestick and silver trumpets which later vanished, possibly in the sack of Rome by the Vandals. Even today, many Jews will avoid walking through the arch that glorifies their tragedy.

From this end of the Forum a slope leads up to the **Palatine Hill**, Rome's legendary birthplace and today its most romantic garden, dotted with toppled columns among the wild flowers and spiny acanthus shrubs. At the time of the Republic, this was a desirable residential district for the wealthy and aristocratic, with Cicero and Crassus among its distinguished inhabitants. Augustus began the Imperial trend and later emperors added and expanded, each trying to oudo the last in magnificence and luxury until the whole area was one immense palace (the very word takes its name from the hill). From the pavilions and terraces of the 16th-century botanical gardens laid out here by the Farnese family, there is an excellent view of the whole Forum.

The so-called **House of Livia** is now believed to be that of her husband, Emperor Augustus, who here combined modesty with taste. Small, graceful rooms retain remnants of mosaic floors and a well-preserved wall painting which depicts Zeus's love for a young priestess. Nearby, a circular Iron Age dwelling unearthed from the time of Rome's legendary beginnings is known as **Casa di Romolo** (Romulus' Hut).

A subterranean passageway linking the palaces, the **Cryptoporticus of Nero**, threads through the Palatine. In the dim light you can just make out stucco decorations on the ceilings and walls. The vast assemblage of ruins of the Domus Flavia include a basilica, throne room, banqueting hall, baths, porticoes, and a fountain in the

Graceful statues of ancient Rome's maiden princesses line the Hall of Vestal Virgins.

The detailed friezes of Trajan's Column are a veritable textbook of Roman warfare.

form of a maze. Together with the Domus Augustana, the complex is known as the **Palace of Domitian**. From one side you can look down into the **Stadium of Domitian,** which was probably a venue for horse races, but thought by some to have been a sunken garden.

The last emperor to build on the Palatine, Septimius Severus, carried the imperial palace right to the southeastern end of the hill, so that his seven-storeyed **Domus Severiana** was the impressive first glimpse of the capital for new arrivals. It was dismantled and its vast expanses of marble used to build Renaissance Rome, and only the huge arcaded fountains remain.

From this edge of the Palatine you have a splendid view down into the immense grassy stretch of the **Circus Maximus**, where crowds of up to 200,000 watched chariot races from tiers of marble seats.

The **Imperial Forums** were built as an adjunct to the Foro Romano in honour of Julius Caesar, Augustus, Trajan, Vespasian, and Nerva. The most impressive monument is the 30 metre (98 foot) **Trajan's Column** (A.D. 113). Celebrating Trajan's campaigns against the Dacians in what is now Romania, the minutely detailed friezes spiralling round the Column constitute a veritable textbook of Roman warfare, featuring embarkation on ships, the clash of armies, and the surrender of Barbarian chieftains. St. Peter's statue replaced the emperor's in 1587.

The Colosseum

It says something about the essential earthiness of Rome that, more than any inspirational church or palace, it is the **Colosseum**—Byron called it "the gladiator's bloody circus"—that is the symbol of the city's eternity. Built in A.D. 72-80 by 20,000 slaves and prisoners, the four-tiered elliptical amphitheatre seated 50,000 spectators on stone benches according to social status.

Flowing in and out of 80 arched passageways known as *vomitoria*, aristocrat and plebeian alike came to see blood: bears, lions, tigers, and leopards starved into attacking one another; trained fighters slaying animals; gladiators butchering one another to cries of "*Jugula!*" ("Slit his throat!"). The gladiators were originally criminals, war captives, and slaves; later, free men entered the "profession," tempted by wealth and fame. Contrary to popular belief, there is little historical evidence to support the image of the Colosseum as the place where Christians were fed to the lions.

Popes and princes have since stripped the Colosseum of its precious marble, travertine, and metal for their churches and palaces. They have left behind a ruined maze of cells and corridors which funnelled both men and beasts to the slaughter. The horror has disappeared beneath the moss, but the thrill of the monument's endurance remains. As an old Anglo-Saxon prophecy goes: "While stands the Colosseum, Rome shall stand; when falls the Colosseum, Rome shall fall; and when Rome falls with it shall fall the world."

The nearby **Arch of Constantine** celebrates Constantine's victory over his imperial rival Maxentius at the Mulvian Bridge. He may have won the battle, but a cost-conscious Senate took fragments from monuments of earlier rulers Trajan, Hadrian, and Marcus Aurelius to decorate the arch.

The huge third-century **Terme di Caracalla** (Baths of Caracalla), 1 km (½ mile south of the Colosseum, were built for 1,600 people to bathe in considerable style and luxury. Public bathing was a prolonged social event as merchants and senators passed from the *caldarium* (hot room) to cool down in the *tepidarium* and the *frigidarium*. The baths ran dry in the sixth century when Barbarians cut the aqueducts. Until 1994, the massive *caldarium* was the stage of spectacular open-air operas, now banned to protect the site. If adequate measures can be found to protect the ancient baths, it is possible that the ban will be lifted.

Seeing the Pope

When he's not in Bogotá or Bangkok, it is possible to see the Pope in person at his personal residence, the Vatican. He normally holds a public audience every Wednesday at 11am (10am in summer), either in a large modern audience hall or down in St. Peter's Square (and sometimes at his summer residence at Castel Gandolfo). An invitation to a papal audience may be obtained from the Pontifical Prefect's Office (open Monday to Saturday in the morning; tel. 69883273) through the bronze gates in St. Peter's Square. It's advisable to book two weeks in advance. A visitor's bishop at home can arrange a private audience.

On Sundays at noon, the Pope appears at the window of his apartments in the Apostolic Palace (right of the basilica, overlooking the square), delivers a brief homily, says the Angelus and blesses the crowd below. On a few major holy days, the pontiff celebrates high mass in St. Peter's.

THE VATICAN

The power of Rome endures both in the spirituality evoked by every stone in St. Peter's Basilica and in the physical awe inspired by the splendours of the Vatican palace. At their best, the popes and cardinals replaced military conquest by moral leadership and persuasion; at their worst, they could show the same hunger for political power and wealth as any caesar. A visit to the Vatican is an object lesson for faithful and sceptic alike.

Constantine, first Christian emperor, erected the original St. Peter's Basilica over an oratory on the site of the Apostle's tomb in 324. After it was sacked in 846 by marauding Saracens, Pope Leo IV ordered massive walls to be built around the sacred church, and the enclosed area became known as the Leonine City—and later the Vatican City, after the Etruscan name of its hill.

The Vatican became the main residence of the popes only after 1378, when the papacy was returned to Rome from exile in Avignon (see page 18). It has been a sovereign state, independent of Italy, since the Lateran Pact signed with Mussolini in 1929. The Pope is supreme ruler of this tiny state, which is guarded by an elite corps of Swiss Guards, founded in 1506, who still wear the blue, scarlet, and orange uniforms said to have been designed by Michelangelo. The papal domain has its own newspaper, *L'Osservatore Romano*, and a radio station which broadcasts worldwide. It also has shops, banks, a minuscule railway station (rarely used), and a post office that will get your postcards home far more quickly than the Italian postal service.

Apart from the 1 square km (½ square mile) comprising St. Peter's Square, St. Peter's Basilica, and the papal palace and gardens, the Vatican also has jurisdiction over other, extra-territorial enclaves, including the basilicas of St. John Lateran, Santa Maria Maggiore, and St. Paul's, as well as the Pope's summer residence at Castel Gandolfo (see page 82).

You don't need a passport to cross the border, and in fact you hardly even notice that you have—though it is marked by a band of white travertine stones running from the ends of the two colonnades at the rim of St. Peter's Square. The Vatican Tourist Information Office on St. Peter's Square arranges guided tours and issues tickets to the grounds of the Vatican City, including the gardens. From here buses go regularly, bound for the Vatican Museums.

A visit to St. Peter's combines ideally with a tour of the Castel Sant'Angelo, culminating in a picnic and siesta on the nearby Janiculum Hill. It is best to save the Vatican Museums for a separate day.

Castel Sant'Angelo

Cross the Tiber by the **Ponte Sant'Angelo**, which incorporates arches of Hadrian's original bridge, the Pons Aelius. Ten windswept angles designed by Bernini, each bearing a symbol of the Passion of Christ, adorn the balustrades.

From the bridge you have the best view of the cylindrical bulk of the **Castel Sant'Angelo**, its mighty brick walls stripped of their travertine and pitted by cannonballs, but nevertheless standing up well to the ravages of time. Conceived by Hadrian around A.D. 130 as his family mausoleum, it became part of the defensive Aurelian Wall a century later. The castle gained its present name in A.D. 590 after Pope Gregory the Great had a vision of the Archangel Michael alighting on a turret and sheathing his sword to signal the end of a plague. For centuries this was Rome's mightiest military bastion and a refuge for the popes in times of trouble; Clement VII holed up here during the sack of Rome by Habsburg troops in 1527.

A spiral ramp, showing traces of the original black-and-white mosaic paving, leads up to the funerary chamber where the ashes of emperors were kept in urns. You emerge

In times of crisis, beleaguered popes took refuge behind the stout walls of the Castel Sant'Angelo.

into the **Cortile dell'Angelo** (Court of the Angel), which is stacked neatly with cannonballs and watched over by a marble angel. An arms museum opens off the courtyard.

After the grimness of the exterior, it comes as a surprise to step into the luxurious surroundings of the old **Papal Apartments**. Lavish frescoes cover the walls and ceilings of rooms hung with masterpieces by Dosso Dossi, Nicolas Poussin, and Lorenzo Lotto. Off the Courtyard of Alexander VI is possibly the most exquisite bathroom in history. The tiny room, just wide enough for its marble bathtub, is painted with delicate designs over every inch of its walls and along the side of the bath.

A harsh jolt brings you back to reality as you enter the **dungeons**, scene of torture and executions. You have to bend over double to get into the bare, stone cells where famous

The sweeping curves of colonnades around Piazza San Pietro reach out to Rome and the whole world.

prisoners languished—among them sculptor-goldsmith Benvenuto Cellini and philosopher Giordano Bruno.

The **Gallery of Pius IV**, surrounding the entire building, affords tremendous views in all directions, as does the terrace on the summit, with the 18th-century bronze *Statue of St. Michael* by Verschaffelt. Opera lovers will recall this as the stage for the final act of Puccini's *Tosca*, in which the heroine hurls herself to her death from the battlements.

St. Peter's

From the Castel Sant'Angelo a wide, straight avenue, the Via della Conciliazione, leads triumphantly up to St. Peter's. A maze of medieval streets, in which stood Raphael's studio, was destroyed in the 1930s to provide an unobstructed view of St. Peter's all the way from the banks of the Tiber. A thick wall running parallel to the avenue conceals a passageway (*Il Passetto*) linking the Vatican to the Castel Sant'Angelo, by which the fleeing popes reached their bastion in safety.

In **Piazza San Pietro** (St. Peter's Square), his greatest creation, Bernini managed to conceive one of the world's most exciting pieces of architectural orchestration. The sweeping curves of the colonnades reach out to Rome and the whole world, *urbi et orbi*, to draw the flood of pilgrims into the bosom of the church. On Easter Sunday as many as 300,000 people cram into the piazza. The square is on or near the site of Nero's Circus, where early Christians were martyred.

Bernini completed the 284 travertine columns and 88 pilasters topped by 140 statues of the saints in just 11 years, from 1656 to 1667. In the centre of the ellipse rises a 25 metre (82 foot) red granite **obelisk**, brought here from Egypt by Caligula in A.D. 37. Stand on one of the two circular paving stones set between the obelisk and the twin 17th-century fountains to see the quadruple rows of perfectly aligned Doric columns appear magically as one.

By any standards a grandiose achievement, **St. Peter's Basilica** does inevitably suffer from the competing visions of all the architects called in to collaborate—Bramante, Baldassare Peruzzi, Giuliano da Sangallo, Carlo Maderno, Giacomo della Porta, Raphael, Michelangelo, and Domenico Fontana, each of whom added, subtracted, and modified, often with a pope over his shoulder.

From 1506, when the new basilica was begun under Julius II, until 1626 when it was consecrated, St. Peter's Basilica was to change form several times. It started out as a simple Greek cross, with four arms of equal length, as favoured by Bramante and Michelangelo, and ended up as Maderno's Latin cross extended by a long nave, as demanded by the popes of the Counter-Reformation. One result is that Maderno's porticoed façade and nave obstruct a clear view of Michelangelo's dome from the square.

Stepping into the basilica is "like entering eternity," according to Goethe. The world's largest Roman Catholic church certainly has immense dimensions: 212 metres (695 feet) long on the outside, 187 metres (613 feet) inside, and 132 metres (435 feet) to the tip of the dome. Brass markers on the floor of the central aisle show how far other famous cathedrals fail to measure up.

You'll find the basilica's most worthy artistic treasure, Michelangelo's sublime *Pietà*, in its own chapel to the right of the entrance. The artist was only 24 when he executed this deeply moving marble sculpture of the Virgin cradling the crucified Christ in her lap. This is the only work which he bothered to sign (on the Madonna's sash), after overhearing people crediting it to another sculptor. Since the statue was attacked by a religious fanatic with a hammer in 1972, it has been protected by a glass screen. Reverence can also cause damage: on the 13th-century bronze *Statue of St. Peter*, a work of the Florentine architect-sculptor Arnolfo di Cambio, the toes have been worn away by the lips and fingers of countless pilgrims.

Beneath the dome, Bernini's great *baldacchino* (canopy) soars over the high altar, at which only the Pope may celebrate mass. The canopy and four spiralling columns were cast from bronze beams taken from the Pantheon (see page 38). At the bottom of each column are a coat of arms bearing the three bees of the Barberini Pope Urban VIII, who commissioned the work. In the apse is an even more extravagant Baroque work, Bernini's bronze and marble *Cathedra of St. Peter*, throne of the Apostle's successors, into which is supposedly incorporated the wooden chair of St. Peter.

For his imposing **dome**, Michelangelo drew inspiration from the Pantheon and the cathedral in Florence. A lift takes you as far as the gallery above the nave, from where there is a dizzying view down into the interior of the basilica, as well as close-ups of the inside of the dome. Spiral stairs and ramps lead on and up to the outdoor balcony which circles the top of the dome for stunning views of the Vatican City and all Rome.

The **Vatican Grottoes** beneath the basilica harbour the tombs of popes and numerous little chapels, some decorated by such masters as Melozzo da Forlì, Giotto, and Pollaiulo. The **necropolis**, even deeper underground, shelters several pre-Christian tombs, as well as a simple monument which may have marked St. Peter's burial place. This excavated area is not open to general viewing and visits should be arranged in advance through the Ufficio Scavi (excavations office, which you'll find just beyond the Arco della Campana to the left of the basilica).

St. Peter's is open daily from 7:00 A.M. to 6:00 P.M. (until 7:00 P.M. from June to September). Masses are said frequently in the side chapels, in various languages. Visitors wearing shorts, bare-backed dresses, or other scanty attire are politely turned away.

Vatican Museums

It should come as no surprise that the Catholic Church, as the greatest patron that painters, sculptors, and architects have known, should have in its headquarters one of the richest collections of art in the world. The 7 km (4 miles) of rooms and galleries of the **Vatican Museums** offer a microcosm of Western civilization. There is an almost bewildering profusion, from Egyptian mummies, Etruscan gold jewellery, and Greek and Roman sculpture, through Renaissance and medieval masterpieces to modern religious art. On a single ticket you can visit eight museums, five galleries, the Apostolic Library, Borgia Apartments, Raphael Rooms, and, of course, the Sistine Chapel.

*An endless array of treasures and antiquities awaits
visitors to the Vatican Museum.*

Once past the entrance, you ascend a wide spiral ramp,
and then choose between four colour-coded itineraries which
range from 1½ hours (A, violet) to 5 hours (D, yellow). The
following gives a selection of some of the highlights.

With the booty from the ruthless dismantling of ancient
monuments to make way for the Renaissance city in the 16th
century, the **Museo Pio-Clementino** has assembled a wonderful collection of classical art. The most celebrated piece
is the first-century B.C. *Laocoön* group of the Trojan priest
and his sons, who were strangled by serpents for offending
Apollo. Famous during Imperial times, it was unearthed
from a vineyard on the Esquiline in 1506, to the delight of

Michelangelo, who rushed to view it. It now stands in a recess of the charming octagonal Belvedere courtyard.

Roman copies of some other Greek sculptures, such as the *Aphrodite of Cnidos* of Praxiteles and the superb *Apollo Belvedere*, achieved a fame as great as the originals, which are now sadly lost. Take note in particular of the powerful muscular *Torso* by Apollonius, which had a profound influence on Renaissance artists and sculptors.

The **Gregorian-Etruscan Museum** displays the exciting finds from a Seventh-century B.C. Etruscan burial mound at Cerveteri (see page 83), whose tomb yielded an abundance of treasures. Among the fine jewellery is a gold brooch surprisingly decorated with lions and ducklings. Look out for the striking bronze statue of a sprightly Etruscan warrior, the *Mars of Todi* (fourth century B.C.).

Judging by the number of obelisks scattered throughout Rome, Egyptian art was much admired and sought after by the ancient Romans. The basis of the collection in the **Egyptian Museum** rests on finds from Rome and its surroundings, particularly from the Gardens of Sallust between the Pincian and Quirinal hills, the Temple of Isis on the Campus Martius, and Hadrian's Villa at Tivoli (see page 80). One of the rooms recreates the underground chamber of a tomb in the Valley of the Kings.

Pope Julius II took a calculated risk in 1509 when he called in a relatively untried 26-year-old to decorate his new residence. The result was the four **Stanze di Raffaello** (Raphael Rooms). In the central Stanza della Segnatura are the two masterly frescoes, *Disputation over the Holy Sacrament* and the *School of Athens*, which contrasted theological and philosophical wisdom.

The *Disputation* unites biblical figures with historical pillars of the faith such as Pope Gregory, Thomas Aquinas, and other pillars of the faith, and the painter Fra Angelico and the divine Dante as well. At the centre of the *School*, Raphael is believed to have given the red-robed Plato the features of Leonardo da Vinci, while portraying Michelangelo as the thoughtful Heraclitus, seated in the foreground.

For a stark contrast to Raphael's grand manner, seek out the gentle beauty of Fra Angelico's frescoes in the **Cappella del Beato Angelico** (Chapel of Nicholas V). The lives of saints Lawrence and Stephen are told in delicately subdued pinks and blues, highlighted with gold.

The richly decorated **Borgia Apartments** contain Pinturicchio's sublime frescoes, with portraits of lusty Pope Alexander VI and his notorious son Cesare and daughter Lucrezia, and lead into the modern religious art collection of Paul VI. This includes Matisse's Madonna sketches, Rodin bronzes, Picasso ceramics, designs for ecclesiastical robes and, somewhat unexpectedly, a grotesque pope by Francis Bacon.

One of Europe's finest collections of ancient manuscripts and rare books is kept in the hallowed precincts of the **Apo-**

Working Solo on the Ceiling

As might be imagined, painting the Sistine ceiling wasn't easy. Michelangelo, a sculptor who used marble and had only a limited experience of oil painting, had never before produced a fresco. Preferring his inexperience to their incompetence, he fired his seven assistants in the first couple of weeks and continued alone for four years, from 1508 to 1512. Contrary to legend, he did not lie on his back, but painted erect on tiptoe, bent backwards "like a Syrian bow," with Pope Julius II climbing the scaffolding to check on progress and threatening to throw him off his platform if he didn't hurry up.

"I'm not in a good place," he wrote to a friend, "and I'm no painter."

Prior to creating his masterpiece on the ceiling of the Sistine Chapel, Michelangelo had never before produced a fresco.

stolic Library. In the great vaulted reading room, or Sistine Hall, designed by Domenico Fontana in 1588, walls and ceilings are covered with paintings of ancient libraries, conclaves, thinkers, and writers. Showcases displaying precious illuminated manuscripts have replaced the old lecterns. A 1,600-year-old copy of Virgil's works, the poems of Petrarch, a sixth-century gospel of St. Matthew, and Henry VIII's love letters to Anne Boleyn are among the prize possessions.

Nothing can prepare you for the visual shock of the **Cappella Sistina** (Sistine Chapel), built for Sixtus IV in the 15th century. Despite the distracting presence of the crowds, visitors seem to yield to the power of Michelangelo's ceiling, his *Last Judgement*, as well as the other wall frescoes of Botticelli, Rosselli, Pinturicchio, Ghirlandaio, and Signorelli. In this private papal chapel, where cardinals hold their conclave to elect the new Pope, the glory of the Catholic Church achieves its finest artistic expression.

The chapel portrays nothing less than the story of man, in three parts: from Adam to Noah; the giving of the Law to Moses; and from the birth of Jesus to the Last Judgement. Towards the centre of the ceiling you can make out the celebrated outstretched finger of the *Creation of Adam*. Most overwhelming of all, particularly now that the colours are so fresh and vivid after a recent restoration, is the impression of the whole. This is best appreciated looking back from the bench by the chapel's exit.

On the chapel's altar wall is Michelangelo's tempestuous *Last Judgement*, painted 23 years after the ceiling, when the artist was in his sixties, and imbued with profound religious soul-searching. An almost naked Jesus dispenses justice more like a stern, even fierce classical god-hero than the conventionally gentle biblical figure. The artist's agonizing self-portrait can be seen in the flayed skin of St. Bartholomew, below Jesus.

Amid all the Vatican's treasures, the 15 rooms of the **Pinacoteca Vaticana** (Picture Gallery), in a separate wing of the palace, sometimes get short shrift. Among the most important exhibits in this collection, covering ten centuries of painting, are works by Fra Angelico, Perugino, Raphael's *Transfiguration* (his last great work), Leonardo da Vinci's unfinished *St. Jerome* in sombre tones of sepia, Bellini's *Pietà*, and Caravaggio's *Descent from the Cross*.

As you wander the galleries, glance out of the windows from time to time to view St. Peter's dome over the clipped hedges of the Vatican gardens (the best views are from the Gallery of the Maps). Take a rest in the **Cortile della Pigna**, dominated by the enormous bronze pinecone fountain (first century A.D.) which gives the courtyard its name.

The Renaissance ceiling of the Santa Maria Maggiore was gilded with the first gold to arrive in Rome from the Americas.

The Janiculum

After absorbing the riches of the Vatican, you could be forgiven for suffering a severe case of cultural overload. Rising above the Vatican, the Janiculum Hill provides prescribed respite in the shade of its parks. There is a breathtaking view of Rome from the **Piazzale Garibaldi** at its crest. In the centre of the square is an equestrian statue of the hero of the Risorgimento, who fought a fierce battle here in 1849. From the crest the road winds down into Trastevere (see page 43).

CHURCHES

It's impossible to list—much less visit—all the churches in Rome. There are some 280 within the centre of the city, far more than even the most zealous of pilgrimages can encompass. Students of history and art, as well as pilgrims, aim to visit, at least, the four patriarchal basilicas: St. Peter's (see page 56), Santa Maria Maggiore, St. John Lateran, and St. Paul's Outside the Walls.

> **When visiting churches, shorts, backless dresses, and tank tops should not be worn.**

Some churches have relics of saints and martyrs to make them special sites, others are significant landmarks in the development of Western architecture, and many more contain magnificent works of art. Here is a representative selection of those that visitors will want to include in an itinerary.

☞ Santa Maria Maggiore

According to a 13th-century legend, this largest and most splendid of all the churches dedicated to the Virgin Mary was built in the fourth century by Pope Liberius after a vision from the Virgin Mary. In fact, it almost certainly dates from 420 and was completed soon afterwards by Pope Sixtus III.

Glittering **mosaics** enhance the perfect proportions of the interior. Above the 40 ancient Ionic columns of the triple nave, a mosaic frieze portrays Old Testament scenes leading to the coming of Christ. The theme is continued in the gilded Byzantine-style mosaics on the triumphal arch, detailing the birth and the childhood of Jesus, and culminates in the magnificent 13th-century portrayal of Mary and Jesus enthroned, in the apse behind the high altar. Inlaid red and green precious marbles pattern the floor in a style first pioneered by Rome's Cosmati family of craftsmen during the 12th century.

The opulent coffered **Renaissance ceiling** was gilded with the first shipment of gold to arrive in Rome from the Americas. A casket of gold, silver, and crystal contains fragments reputed to have come from the holy crib, brought back from the Holy Land by St. Helena, Constantine's mother.

The incomparably rich **Cappella Paolina** (Pauline Chapel) has an altar inlaid with agate, amethyst, and lapis lazuli set beneath a revered ninth-century painting of the Madonna and Child. On 5 August, white petals are showered on the altar to mark the date when a miraculous fall of snow, prophesied by the Virgin, showed Pope Liberius where to build the church.

St. John Lateran

Regarded as the mother church of the Roman Catholic world (it's the seat of the Pope as Bishop of Rome), **San Giovanni in Laterano** pre-dated even the first St. Peter's by a few years. Constantine built both basilicas in the early fourth century.

Popes lived in the Lateran Palace for a thousand years until they moved to Avignon, and then to the Vatican in the 14th century. On a wooden table, incorporated in the high altar, St. Peter himself is said to have celebrated mass.

Fire, earthquake, and looting by the Vandals reduced the church to ruins over the centuries. The present basilica, little more than 300 years old, is at least the fifth on this site. But the bronze **central doors** go all the way back to ancient Rome, when they graced the entrance to the Curia in the Forum (see page 46). High above the basilica's façade, 15 giant white statues of Jesus, John the Baptist, and Church sages stand out against the sky.

Transformed by Borromini in the 17th century, the interior of the church gives a predominant impression of sombre white and grey, more restrained than is usual for Baroque architects. The only exuberant touches are the coloured marble inlays of the paving. In recesses along the nave stand several statues of the Apostles which were sculpted by pupils of Bernini.

The **baptistery** preserves some truly splendid fifth- and seventh-century mosaics. Now octagonal in shape, the original building may have been circular, designed for total immersion and based on Classical models. The beautiful bronze doors of St. John the Baptist's Chapel, removed from the Baths of Caracalla (see page 52), sing musically on their hinges when they are opened.

The brothers Jacopo and Pietro Vassalletto excelled themselves in the **cloisters**, where alternating straight and twisted columns, set in mosaic style, create a perfect setting for meditation.

An ancient edifice opposite the basilica—almost all that's left of the original Lateran Palace—shelters the **Scala Santa**, the holy stairway brought back by St. Helena from Jerusalem and said to have been trodden by Jesus in the house of Pontius Pilate. The devout climb the 28 marble steps on their knees.

Outside the basilica stands an Egyptian **obelisk** brought from the Temple of Ammon in Thebes. It's the tallest in the world—31 metres (102 feet)—and the oldest (1449 B.C.) of the 13 still standing in Rome.

St. Paul's Outside the Walls

St. Paul's Basilica, the largest in Rome after St. Peter's, was built by Constantine in A.D. 314 and enlarged by Valentinian II and Theodosius. Astonishingly, it survived intact until destroyed by fire in 1823. Today, a faithful restoration, though preserving only a little of its former splendour, has recreated **San Paolo fuori le Mura's** original form.

A **tabernacle**, designed by the 13th-century sculptor Arnolfo di Cambio and retrieved from the ashes of the great fire, decorates the high altar under which lies the burial place of St. Paul. After Paul was beheaded, a Roman matron, Lucina, placed the body here in her family vault. Constantine later encased it in a sarcophagus of marble and bronze, looted by Saracen invaders later.

Above the 86 Venetian marble columns runs a row of mosaic medallions representing all the popes from St. Peter to the present day. Pause in the peaceful Benedictine **cloister**, designed by Pietro Vassalletto and surpassing even his work at St. John Lateran. Slender, spiralled columns glitter with green, red, and gold mosaic, enclosing a garden of roses and a gently rippling fountain.

San Clemente

This gem of a church hides a fascinating history which can be traced down through each of its three levels. The present church, dating to the 12th century, is built in basilica form with three naves divided by ancient columns and embellished by a pavement of geometric designs. A symbolic mosaic in the apse features the Cross as the Tree of Life nourishing all living things—birds, animals, and plants.

To the right of the nave, a staircase leads down to the fourth-century **basilica**, which underpins the present church. The Romanesque frescoes, unfortunately, have now drastically faded, but copies show them in the near-perfect condition in which they were uncovered earlier this century.

An ancient stairway leads farther underground to a maze of corridors and chambers, believed to be the home of St. Clement himself, third successor to St. Peter as pope. Also down here is the earliest religious structure on this site, a pagan **temple** (*Mithraeum*) dedicated to the god Mithras. A sculpture shows the Persian god of light slaying a bull. The sound of trickling water from a nearby stream echoes eerily through these subterranean chambers as it drains off into the Cloaca Maxima (see page 42).

Santa Prassede

Though unremarkable from the outside, this little church is enchanting in the intimacy of its interior. St. Praxedes and her sister Pudentiana were the daughters of a Roman senator, who as one of the first converts to Christianity gave shelter to St. Peter.

Delicate ninth-century mosaics of Jesus and four angels glittering with gold cover the **Chapel of St. Zeno**, making it the city's most important Byzantine monument. It was designed as a tomb for Theodora, mother of Pope Paschal I—medieval Romans called it the "Garden of Paradise" because of its beauty. To the right is a fragment of rare jasper, said to have come from the column to which Jesus was tied for his flagellation.

Roof fresco of San Pietro in Vincoli, built on the site where St. Peter was put on trial.

San Pietro in Vincoli

St. Peter in Chains may not attract a second glance (and it might even prefer it that way, given the hordes of visitors) if it didn't contain one of Michelangelo's greatest sculptures, his formidable **Moses**. Intended for St. Peter's as part of Michelangelo's unsuccessful project for Julius II's tomb, the statue of the great biblical figure sits in awesome majesty at the centre of the space. You can imagine how grandiose the original plan must have been when you realize from his sideward stare that Moses was supposed to be just a corner figure facing the centre. The horns on his head continue the traditional medieval mistranslation of the Hebrew for halo-like rays of light. On each side, the comparatively passive figures of Jacob's two wives, a prayerful Rachel and melancholy Leah, were the last completed sculptures of Michelangelo.

Empress Eudoxia founded the church in the fifth century, on the site of the Roman law court where St. Peter was tried and sentenced. It was built as a sanctuary for the chains with which Herod bound St. Peter in Palestine, together with those used when he was imprisoned in Rome. They are kept in a bronze reliquary beneath the high altar.

The Gesù was intended by the Jesuits to wrest popular support from the Protestants.

The Gesù

Severe and relatively discreet on its own piazza west of the Piazza Venezia, the Gesù is the mother church of the Jesuits and was a major element in their Counter-Reformation campaign. Begun as their Roman headquarters in 1568, its open plan became the model for the congregational churches that were intended to wrest popular support from the Protestants. While its façade is more sober than the Baroque churches put up as the movement gained momentum, the **interior** glorifies the newly found militancy in gleaming bronze, gold, marble, and precious stones.

St. Ignatius Loyola, a Spanish soldier who founded the order, has a fittingly magnificent **tomb** under a richly decorated altar in the left transept, with a profusion of lapis lazuli. The globe at the top is said to be the largest piece of this stone in the world.

Sant'Ignazio

In gentler contrast, the nearby church of Sant'Ignazio stands in an enchanting setting of russet and ochre Rococo houses. Inside, Andrea Pozzo (himself a Jesuit priest and designer of the saint's tomb in the Gesù) has painted a superb *trompe-l'oeil* **ceiling fresco** (1685) depicting St. Ignatius's entry into paradise. Stand on a buff stone disk in the nave's central aisle and you will have the extraordinary impression of the whole building rising above you through the ingenious architectural effect of the painting. From any other point, the columns appear to collapse. From another disk farther up the aisle you can admire the celestial dome above the high altar, but as you advance, it begins to take on strange proportions. (See page 118 for opening hours)

MUSEUMS

The Romans have been enthusiastic patrons and collectors of art for millennia, and their museums are packed with treasures. Here are a few of the best (Vatican Museums on p. 59).

Galleria Borghese

The avid and ruthless art collector Cardinal Scipione Borghese conceived this handsome Baroque villa in the Villa Borghese (see page 33) as a home for his small but outstanding collection, using his prestige as the nephew of Pope Paul V to extort coveted masterpieces from their owners.

After extensive restoration—during which only part of the collection has been on view—the Borghese reopened in its entirety in spring of 1997.

The highlights of the collection are several astonishing **sculptures** by the cardinal's young protégé, Bernini. These include busts of his patron; a vigorous *David* (said to be a youthful self-portrait); and a graceful nearby sculpture, *Apollo and Daphne*, in which the water nymph turns into a laurel just as the god is about to seize her. In a later addition, now the star attraction, Antonio Canova portrays Napoleon's sister Pauline, who married into the Borghese family, as a naked reclining Venus.

It's worth looking up to see the intricately painted ceiling in the Galleria Borghese.

There are some exceptional pieces in the collection, including Raphael's *Descent from the Cross*, Titian's *Sacred and Profane Love*, Caravaggio's *David with the Head of Goliath,* and *Madonna of the Serpent*, along with works by Botticelli, Rubens, Dürer, and Cranach.

Villa Giulia

This 16th-century pleasure palace of a pope, northwest of the Villa Borghese, is now the lovely setting for Italy's finest **museum of Etruscan art**. Although much about this pre-Roman civilization is still a mystery, the Etruscans left a wealth of detail about their customs and everyday life by burying the personal possessions of the dead with them in their tombs.

Replicas show the round stone burial mounds, built like huts. Room after room is filled with objects from the tombs: bronze statues of warriors in battledress; shields, weapons, and chariots (even the skeletons of two horses); gold and silver jewellery; decorative vases imported by Etruscans from Greece; and a host of everyday cooking utensils, mirrors, and combs. Note the bronze toilet box adorned with figures of the Argonauts. The highlight is a life-size terra-cotta sculpture, for a sarcophagus lid, of a blissful young couple reclining on a banquet couch.

Museo Nazionale Romano

This superb collection housed in the Roman Baths of Diocletian offers the best intorduction to Rome's Greek and Roman antiquities. Larger even than those of Caracalla, Diocletian's baths covered 120 hectares (300 acres), part of which are now occupied by the Piazza della Repubblica and Michelangelo's church of Santa Maria degli Angeli, near Termini station.

The *piccolo chiostro* (small cloister) of the old Carthusian monastery provides an attractive setting for the magnificent **Ludovisi Collection**, assembled by Cardinal Ludovico Ludovisi in the 17th century. Among the most important pieces is the marble altartop known as the *Ludovisi Throne*, an original Greek work from the fifth century B.C., with exquisitely carved reliefs of Aphrodite and a maiden playing the flute. Also seek out the tragic statue of a Barbarian warrior in the act of killing himself and his wife rather than submit to slavery.

Other highlights include the *Apollo of the Tiber*, a copy of a bronze group by the young Pheidias; a copy, probably the best ever, of Myron's famed *Discobolos* (Discus Thrower); the *Daughter of Niobe*, an original from the fifth century B.C.; the *Venus of Cyrene*; a bronze of a young man leaning on a lance; and a variety of portrait sculptures, including one of Emperor Augustus.

The **landscape frescoes** taken from the imperial villa of Livia show nature at its most bountiful, with flowers, trees, birds, and fruit painted with great attention to detail.

Galleria Nazionale d'Arte Antica

The Palazzo Barberini (on the Via delle Quattro Fontane) provided another architectural battleground for rivals Borromini and Bernini, each of whom built one of its grand staircases and contributed to the superb façade. It is worth a visit as much for its Baroque décor as for its collection of paintings. Iin the palace's **Great Hall** is Pietro da Cortona's dazzling illusionist ceiling fresco, *Triumph of Divine Providence*.

Most of the national art collection is hung in the first-floor gallery (the rest is housed in the **Palazzo Corsini** across the Tiber in Trastevere; see page 43). Works include a Fra Angelico triptych, the famous portrait of King Henry VIII by Hans Holbein, and paintings by Titian, Tintoretto, and El Greco. Look for Raphael's *La Fornarina*, said to be a portrait of his mistress, and Caravaggio's depiction of Judith in the act of severing the head of Holofernes.

Galleria Doria Pamphili

The vast Palazzo Doria in the Corso is still the private residence of the Doria family, but the public are allowed in on Tuesdays, Fridays, Saturdays, and Sundays to view their rich collection of paintings, assembled over hundreds of years. A catalogue is vital, as the paintings are identified by number.

Much of the collection is poorly lit, but there are a number of masterpieces from the 15th through 17th centuries, including works by Titian, Veronese, Raphael, and Caravaggio, as well as from the Dutch and Flemish schools. Look out for the evocative landscape of the *Flight into Egypt* by

Annibale Carracci and the windswept *Naval Battle in the Bay of Naples* by Brueghel the Elder.

You'll find a nice stylistic contrast in a little room off the galleries, which juxtaposes a brilliant worldly portrait by Velázquez of Innocent X, the Pamphili family pope, alongside a more serene marble bust of him by Bernini.

EXCURSIONS

The main excursions into the Roman countryside and Lazio (Latium) are those that ancient Romans took to holiday homes by the sea or nearby hills and lakes. You should take an important short trip just outside the city walls to the Old Appian Way.

Old Appian Way

Heading southeast through the Porta San Sebastiano, look back for a good view of the old **Aurelian Wall**, still enclosing part of Rome. Its massive defensive ramparts stretch into the distance, topped by towers and bastions built to resist the onslaught of Barbarian invasions in the third century.

Ahead lies a narrow lane, hemmed in at first by hedges and the high walls of film stars' and millionaires' homes— the **Old Appian Way**. When Appius Claudius the Censor opened the road and gave it his name in 312 B.C., the Appian Way was the grandest road the Western world had ever known. You can still see some of the original paving stones over which the Roman legions marched on their way to Brindisi to set sail for the Levant and North Africa.

Since by law burials could not take place within the city walls, the tombs of the dead were built along this road. On either side lie the ruins of sepulchres of 20 generations of patrician families, some with simple tablets, others with impressive mausoleums. For the same reason, the Christians built their cemeteries in the catacombs here.

At a fork in the road, the chapel of **Domine Quo Vadis** marks the spot where St. Peter, fleeing Nero's persecution in Rome, is said to have encountered Christ and asked: "*Domine, quo vadis?*" ("Whither goest thou, Lord?"). Christ is believed to have replied: "I go to Rome to be crucified again." Ashamed of his fear, Peter turned back to Rome and his own crucifixion. The little chapel contains a copy of a stone with a footprint said to have been left by Christ (the original is in the Basilica of San Sebastiano).

Farther along the Appia Antica, within a short distance of each other, are three of Rome's most celebrated catacombs: St. Callisto, Domitilla, and St. Sebastian. About six million early Christians, among them many martyrs and saints, were

---

The Third City

The historic centre of Rome has been kept mercifully free of antagonistic 20th-century innovations. But there is an ultra-modern "Third Rome," 5 km (3 miles) south along the Ostian Way, which was Mussolini's dream, intended to rival the glories of the Imperial and Renaissance cities.

Known simply by its initials EUR (pronounced "Ay-oor"), this complex of massive white-marble buildings, with wide avenues and open spaces grouped around an artificial lake, was designed for a world fair in 1942 to mark 20 years of Fascism. The war interrupted construction, however, and the fair never took place.

In recent years, EUR has developed into a thriving township of government ministries, offices, conference centres, and fashionable apartments. Several buildings remain from Mussolini's time, including the formidable cube of arches of the Palazzo della Civiltà del Lavoro (Palace of Workers), known as the "Square Colosseum." For the 1960 Olympics, architect Pier Luigi Nervi designed the huge, domed Palazzo dello Sport.

buried in 50 of these vast cemeteries. Knowledgeable guides accompany you in groups into a labyrinth of damp, musty-smelling tunnels and chambers burrowed into the soft volcanic tufa rock, sometimes six levels deep (claustrophobes should abstain). Paintings and carvings adorn the catacombs with precious examples of early Christian art.

The entrance to the **Catacombs of St. Calisto** lies at the end of an avenue of cypresses. An official tour takes you down to the second level of excavations, where you will see the burial niches, called *loculi*, cut into the rock one above the other on either side of the dark galleries. Occasionally the narrow passages open out into larger chambers, or *cubicula*, where a family would be buried together. One such crypt sheltered the remains of third-century popes; another held the body of St. Cecilia until it was transferred to the church of Santa Cecilia in Trastevere (the statue of the saint lying in a recess is a copy of the one by Stefano Maderno in the church; see page 43).

In the **Catacombs of St. Sebastiano**, the bodies of the apostles Peter and Paul are said to have been hidden for several years during the third-century persecutions. You can still see graffiti in Latin and Greek invoking the two saints.

The **tomb of Cecilia Metella** dominates the Appian landscape. This almost unknown noblewoman was a relative of the immensely rich Crassus, who financed Julius Caesar's early campaigns. A 14th-century Roman family added the castellated parapet when they turned it into a fortress.

Alongside extends the well-preserved **Circus of Maxentius**, built for chariot races in A.D. 309 under the last pagan emperor, who carried out the final wave of Christian persecutions in Rome.

Turn off the Via Appia to visit the **Fosse Ardeatine**, a place of pilgrimage for modern Italians. In March 1944, in retaliation for the killing of 32 German soldiers by the Italian Resistance, the Nazis rounded up at random 335 Italian men (10 for each German and an extra 15 for good measure) and machine-gunned them in the sandpits of the Via Ardeatina. Once the Germans left Rome, a poignant memorial was raised here to the dead, among them a boy of 14 years.

Tivoli

The picturesque town of Tivoli perches on a steep slope amid the woods, streams, and twisted silvery olive trees of the Sabine Hills. Inhabited even in ancient times, when it was known as *Tibur*, Tivoli prospered

The Villa d'Este in Tivoli contains some 500 fountains in its garden paradise.

throughout the Middle Ages and thus preserves interesting Roman remains, as well as medieval churches and its famous Renaissance villa and gardens.

Trains leave Stazione Termini every 15 minutes for Rebibbia terminal (metro line B). Buses make the connection from there to Tivoli. By car the drive takes 1¼ hour (30 km/19 miles) along the old Roman chariot road (since repaved!) of the Via Tiburtina.

Signs:
arrivi–**arrival**
partenza–**departed**

The **Villa d'Este** sprawls along the hillside. From its balconies you can look down on the gardens, which fall away in a series of terraces—a paradise of dark cypresses, fountains (estimated at 500), grottoes, pools, and statues.

Cardinal Ippolito II d'Este conceived this pleasure garden in the 16th century; the architect Pirro Ligorio created it. On the **Terrace of 100 Fountains** water jets splash into a long basin guarded by statues of eagles. The **Organ Fountain**, originally accompanied by organ music, cascades steeply down the rocks. On the lowest level three large, deep pools contrast in their stillness with the rush and roar of water elsewhere. The architect took particular delight in strange fantasies, such as the rows of sphinxes who spurt water from their nipples.

Tucked away at the foot of the hills lie the haunting ruins of **Villa Adriana** (Hadrian's Villa). Spread over 70 hecatres (173 acres), this retirement hideaway of the great builder (the Pantheon, see page 38, and Hadrian's Wall in Britain are among his achievements) was designed to recapture some of the architectural marvels of his empire, especially Greece, which he loved above all else. These travel memoirs for his old age were filled with treasures that have since found their way to museums around the world.

Those arriving at the villa by public bus are dropped off at the main gate and ticket office. Tourist coaches and private cars continue up the drive to the car-park in the grounds. An excellent scale model here will give you an overview of the whole. As you will see, this was more a miniature city than a villa. The monumental baths, separate Greek and Latin libraries, temples, and pavilions together make up the home of a man who drew no distinction between the pleasures of mind and body.

You enter the ruins through the colonnades of the Greek-style **Stoa Poikile** (Painted Portico), which leads to the main imperial residence. Adjoining the palace are guest rooms, their black-and-white mosaic floors still visible, and an underground passageway in which the servants moved about unseen.

The enchanting **Villa dell' Isola**, a pavilion surrounded by a little reflecting pool and circular portico, epitomizes all the magic of the place. To the south, remnants of arches and copies of Greek-style caryatids (statues of females used as pillars) surround the **Pool of Canopus** leading to the sanctuary of the Egyptian god Serapis. Barbarians and museum curators have removed most of the villa's treasures, but a stroll among the remaining pillars, arches, and mosaics in gardens running wild among the olive trees, cypresses, and umbrella pines can be marvellously evocative of a lost world.

Ostia Antica

Excavations continue to uncover fascinating sections of what was once the seaport and naval base of ancient Rome. The long-buried city of Ostia stands at the mouth (*ostium*) of the Tiber, 23 km (14 miles) southwest of the capital on the shores of the Tyrrhenian Sea.

Sea-going vessels were unable to travel inland along the shallow Tiber, so river barges plied back and forth from the port, carrying Rome's supply of food and building materials. During its heyday, Ostia had 100,000 residents and boasted splendid baths, a theatre, temples, and imposing houses.

Ostia's well-preserved ruins, set among cypresses and pines reveal more about daily life and the building methods of ancient Rome than do those of the capital. Excavations since the 19th century have unearthed warehouses, apartments known as *insulae* (islands), and private houses facing out to sea and decorated with mosaics and murals.

The **Piazzale delle Corporazioni** (Square of the Corporations) housed 70 commercial offices round a porticoed central temple to Ceres, goddess of agriculture. Mosaic mottoes and emblems in the pavement tell of the trading of grain factors, caulkers, ropemakers, and shipowners from all over the world. The **theatre** next door, built by Agrippa, is worth the climb up the tiered seats for a panaramic view over the whole ruined city.

As in Rome, the **Forum** was the focus of city life, dominated at one end by the Capitol, a temple dedicated to Jupiter, Juno, and Minerva, and at the other by the Temple of Rome and Augustus, with the Curia (seat of the municipal authorities) and the basilica, or law courts, lying between.

To see a typical residence, visit the **House of Cupid and Psyche**, with its rooms paved in marble built round a central garden courtyard. Nearby a small **museum** traces Ostia's history through statues, busts, and frescoes.

The modern seaside resort of Lido di Ostia attracts weekending Romans, who flock to the grey-sand beaches. Swimming is not recommended because of pollution. To compensate, dine in one of the cheerful open-air restaurants.

The Alban Hills and Castel Gandolfo

Immediately to the southeast of Rome, the scattered hilltowns known as the Castelli Romani (Roman Castles) began as fortified refuges during medieval civil wars. Today, it is just the summer heat that drives Romans out on daytrips to the vineyards here.

The Pope's official summer home is at **Castel Gandolfo**, above Lake Albano, where he relaxes in the huge palace designed by Carlo Maderno, set in beautiful landscaped gardens. On summer Wednesdays the Pope no longer holds audience here, but flies by helicopter to the Vatican for his usual appearance. The palace, gardens, and Vatican Observatory in the grounds are closed to visitors. A terrace near the papal palace looks down on the deep, dark blue waters of **Lake Albano**, lying in an old forested volcanic crater below.

The towns of Frascati, Grottaferrata, Marino, and Rocca di Papa make delightful stops, not least for a cool glass of their estimable white wine (especially during the autumn grape harvests).

Castel Gandolfo, overlooking the dark blue waters of Lake Albano, houses the summer retreat of the Pope.

Cerveteri

If the Villa Giulia in Rome (see page 73) and the Gregorian-Etruscan Museum in the Vatican (see page 61) have aroused your curiosity about the Etruscans, it is worth making a trip to the ancient **necropolis** at Cerveteri, 43 km (27 miles) northwest of Rome. Known in ancient times as Caere, it was one of the original 12 towns of the powerful Etruscan League, though it declined in the third century B.C. after becoming a Roman dependency.

The scores of **tombs** here represent every kind of burial from the early shaft and pit graves to *tumuli*, dating from the seventh to first centuries B.C. Stucco decorations and rock carvings represent the weapons, domestic animals, and even household pots and pans that Etruscans felt they would need in the afterlife.

The **Museo Nazionale di Cerveteri**, housed in a 16th-century castle, displays chronologically a rich collection of objects from the tombs, including sarcophagi, sculptures, and wall paintings.

WHAT TO DO

ENTERTAINMENT

Rome offers a wealth of evening entertainments, particularly in the summer months when the balmy evenings entice everyone outdoors. You can choose from the hottest of discos and nightclubs to the coolest of classical music, not to mention lively street festivals full of dancing, fireworks, and open-air dining. Rome's popular summer festival, *L'Estate Romana*, runs from June to September and offers music, film, dance, and theatre in venues across the city, many of them open air.

Concerts of **classical music** are performed in a number of picturesque and historic settings, including the Campidoglio (see page 27), the Isola Tiberina (see page 41), and the cloister of Santa Maria della Pace. The ruins of the Baths of Caracalla (see page 52) are the spectacular location for a summer season of **opera and ballet**. Military and civilian bands perform free concerts in the Pincio gardens (see page 33) from late April to mid-July. **Music clubs** also abound in Rome, with all kinds of music ranging from jazz, blues, and folk to rock, reggae, and salsa.

Cinemas will usually dub foreign-language films into Italian. Exceptions are the Pasquino in Trastevere, the Majestic (on Mondays), the Augustus (on Tuesdays), and the Alcazar (on Mondays).

For up-to-the-minute information about what's going on in Rome, consult the entertainment supplement *Trovaroma* in the Thursday edition of *La Repubblica* newspaper and the weekly *Roma C'è*. The *Carnet di Roma* is a monthly guide to events in and around the city, produced by Rome's Tourist Board (see page 126).

SHOPPING

Italy's great visual culture combining a long artisan tradition and modern design flair come together to make shopping in

The Police Band strikes up a tune on the Salinata della Trinità dei Monti (Spanish Steps).

Rome a delight. You won't necessarily find bargain-basement prices, but you will get superb quality and excellent service.

Where to Shop

The most fashionable shopping district in Rome lies between Piazza di Spagna and Via del Corso. The best in high fashion, jewellery, silk, and leather is to be found in the elegant shops of Via Condotti and its neighbouring streets such as Via Borgognona, Via Frattina, and Via Bocca di Leone.

Via Cola di Rienzo, on the right bank of the river Tiber, not far from the Vatican, is a less exclusive shopping street, but its stores offer excellent quality. Via Nazionale, Via del

Tritone, and Via del Corso are less expensive places to shop for both fashionable clothes and leather.

Specialist shops which are often family-run and generations old are the rule in Rome. You won't find here the grand department stores boasted by other capital cities. The best of Rome's few big stores are Coin (Piazzale Appio, near St. John Lateran) and La Rinascente (main branch at Piazza Colonna). More downmarket alternatives are the Standa and Upim chains, with branches throughout the city. All these have the advantage of longer opening hours than some of the smaller shops.

Signs:
saldi–**on sale**

Be prepared to haggle if you go to Porta Portese, Rome's famous **flea market** held on Sunday morning in the streets and alleys running beside Via Portuense in

The Porta Portese flea market, where you'll find plenty to haggle about on Sunday mornings.

Calendar of Events

January
- 5-6 Jan—*Befana* (Epiphany)—Festival on Piazza Navona
- 21 Jan—Blessing of lambs at Sant'Agnese, Via Nomentana

February/March
- Carnival—Period preceding Lent marked by masked processions and parades

March
- 9 Mar—*Festa di San Francesco Romana*— at Piazzale del Colosseo for blessing

March-April
- Good Friday—the Pope leads the Procession of the Cross at 9pm from the candlelit Colosseum to the Forum
- Easter Sunday—the Pope blesses the crowds from the balcony of St. Peter's at noon

April-May
- *Festa della Primavera* (Spring Festival)— the Spanish Steps flow with pink azaleas
- 21 April— Rome's founding

June
- 29 June—*Festa di San Pietro e San Paolo*— solemn rites in St. Peter's Square

July
- *Noiantri* festival in Trastevere

August
- 5 Aug—*Festa della Madonna della Neve* in Santa Maria Maggiore
- 15 Aug—*Ferragosto* or Feast of the Assumption

September
- Open-air art exhibition in Via Margutta

December
- Cultural Heritage Week—free admission to state museums and monuments (first week)
- Children's toy fair on Piazza Navona (until 6 Jan)
- 8 December—*Festa della Madonna Immacolata* (Immaculate Conception)
- 24 December—the Pope celebrates midnight mass at St. Peter's Basilica

Fashion is everywhere in Rome, from runways to shop windows.

Trastevere. Here you will find new and old clothes, antique bric-à-brac, furniture, jewellery, and books, as well as the odd pickpocket, so take care.

The large **outdoor market** in Via Sannio (near St. John Lateran) is good for bargain clothes. (Every morning except Sundays.) Piazza Vittorio Emanuele II (near Santa Maria Maggiore) has a colourful food market as well as stalls selling clothes and fabrics.

What to Buy

Antiques: It's no surpise to find antiques dealers by the score in a city 2,700 years old. Rome's dealers sell exquisite (but expensive) silver, glass, porcelain, furniture, and paintings. The best antiques shops are in Via del Babuino and Via Margutta (between the Spanish Steps and the Piazza del Popolo), Via Giulia (behind Palazzo Farnese), and Via dei Coronari, historically known as the Street of the Rosary Makers (near Piazza Navona).

Buy antiques or art works only from a reputable dealer, who will provide a certificate of guarantee and obtain the necessary government permit for export.

Books and prints: The market at Largo Fontanella di Borghese (off Via del Corso) specializes in original and reproduction prints and books.

Ceramics: Colourful, attractively designed carafes, jugs, plates, bowls, and tiles are available. Myricae in Via Frattina is good for reasonably priced regional handicrafts.

Fashion: Rome is second to none when it comes to stylish high-fashion clothes. All the famous names of Italian *alta moda* are represented in the Piazza di Spagna area. Look out for Giorgio Armani, Fendi, Valentino, Krizia, and Max Mara.

You'll also find elegantly tailored men's clothes, both custom-made and ready-to-wear. La Cicogna, which has branches throughout the city, provides beautiful clothes for children.

Food and wine: Good gastronomic delicacies to take home with you include cheese (fresh Parmesan), salami, the Parma and San Daniele ham (*prosciutto crudo*), "extra virgin" olive oil, wines from the Castelli Romani, and fiery *grappa*.

Ai Monasteri in Piazza delle Cinque Lune (near Piazza Navona) sells liqueurs, confectionery, olive oil, honey, and other products made by Italian monks.

Jewellery: You'll find fine antique jewellery in Rome, as well as modern designs and costume jewellery. For sheer opulence, nothing can quite match the elegant premises of Bulgari in Via Condotti.

Leather: Stylish leather goods—shoes, handbags, wallets, luggage, and gloves—abound. You'll find Ferragamo and Campanile in Via Condotti.

Textiles: Beautiful silks, colourful knitwear, and hand-embroidered table linen are supplied by Rome's shops. Cesari sells luxurious furnishing fabrics in Via del Babuino and linens in Via Barberini.

EATING OUT

Do as the Romans do and turn your eating out into an evening out. Romans like to spend hours over a leisurely meal of innumerable courses in the genial company of friends in one of the *trattorie* or restaurants which abound in the city. Now that traffic has been banned from large sections of Rome's historic centre, outdoor dining on balmy summer evenings can once more be a delight.

Choice spots are Trastevere (see page 43), around the Campo dei Fiori and the old Jewish ghetto (see page 39), and the Piazza Navona (see page 37). You should also take time to drive out at least once into the countryside beyond the walls to lunch or dine in one of the restaurants along the Via

Go just about anywhere in Rome to find a traditional slice of pizza in a mind-blowing range of varieties.

Appia Antica or the roads to the Alban Hills (see page 82) or Ostia (see page 81).

WHERE TO EAT

Only in some hotels will you find an English or American-style breakfast. Otherwise, go to a good *caffè* on the piazza and settle happily for the *prima colazione* of superb coffee, *espresso* (black), or *cappuccino* (with foaming hot milk), accompanied by a delicious sweet *cornetto* (croissant).

For a quick snack at lunchtime, choose a *tavola calda*, a stand-up bar serving a variety of hot and cold dishes throughout the day, to take away or eat on the spot. You can also have delicious sandwiches made up for you at a local delicatessen (*pizzichieria*). Ask for *panino ripieno*, a bread roll filled with whichever sausage, cheese, or salad you choose from the inviting display on the counter.

> **Male waiters are called *cameriere* (kahmayreeairay), female *cameriera* (kahmayreeairah).**

Fast-food restaurants have been springing up all over Rome in the last few years. More and more ethnic eating places have also been appearing in the city. Chinese restaurants are particularly noticeable, but you can also try African, Arab, Greek, Indian, Japanese, Lebanese, and Mexican cuisines. Vegetarian restaurants are still thin on the ground, but gaining in popularity.

In theory, a *ristorante* is usually a larger and more elaborate establishment than a family-style *trattoria* or rustic *osteria*. But in Rome the distinction is blurred beyond all recognition; thus one of the grandest and priciest restaurants in the city may call itself a humble *osteria*.

The price should not be taken as an indication of the quality of the cuisine; an expensive restaurant may offer a superb meal with service to match, but you may also be paying primarily for the location. Only a few steps away from such famous tourist spots as the Piazza del Popolo and Piazza Navona, you'll find numerous *trattorie* with lower prices, where the ambience, such an important aspect of an Italian meal, is much more appealing and the food has real character.

Restaurants are obliged to display the menu with prices in the window or just inside the door, so you will have an idea of what's on offer before you take the plunge.

WHEN TO EAT

Roman restaurants serve lunch from 12:30 to 3:00 P.M. and dinner from 8:00 P.M. to 11:00 P.M. Some offer late-night supper and are open until 1:00, 2:00, or 3:00 A.M. Each restaurant is closed one day a week, which will vary. If you are set on a particular venue, it is advisable to book by telephone, especially for peak hours (around 1:30 P.M. and 9:00 P.M.).

WHAT TO EAT

Antipasti: Any *trattoria* worth its olive oil will set out on a long table near to the entrance a truly artistic display of its antipasti (*hors d'oeuvre*). The best way to get to know the delicacies is to make up your own assortment (*antipasto misto*). Both attractive to look at and tasty are the cold *peperoni*: red, yellow, and green peppers grilled, skinned, and then marinated in olive oil and a little lemon juice.

Mushrooms (*funghi*), courgettes (*zucchini*), eggplant (*melanzane*), artichokes (*carciofi*), and fennel (*finocchio*) also come cold, with a dressing (*pinzimonio*). One of the most refreshing antipasti is *mozzarella alla caprese*, slices of soft *mozzarella* cheese and tomato in a dressing of fresh basil and olive oil. Ham from Parma or San Daniele is paper thin, served with melon (*prosciutto con melone*) or, even better, fresh figs (*con fichi*).

The Pantheon provides a timeless backdrop for eating out in the Piazza della Rotunda.

Soups: Popular soups are mixed vegetable (*minestrone*), clear soup (*brodo*), and an interesting version with an egg beaten into it (*stracciatella*).

Pasta: Traditionally served as an introductory course, not the main dish. Even the friendliest of restaurant owners will raise a sad eyebrow if you decide to make a whole meal out of a plate of spaghetti. It is said that there are as many different forms of Italian pasta as there are French cheeses—360 at the

Antipasti: the best way to get to know the local delicacies is to make up your own assortment ("antipasto misto").

last count, with new forms created every year. Each sauce— tomato, cheese, cream, meat, or fish— needs its own noodle.

Besides spaghetti and macaroni, the worldwide popularity of pasta has familiarized us with *tagliatelle* ribbon noodles (known here as *fettuccine*), baked *lasagne* with layers of pasta, meat sauce, and béchamel, rolled *cannelloni*, and *ravioli*. From there, you launch into the lusty poetry of *tortellini* and *cappelletti* (variations on *ravioli*), or curved *linguine*, flat *pappardelle*, quill-shaped *penne,* and corrugated *rigatoni*. Discover the other 350 for yourselves.

Furthermore, there are almost as many sauces for pasta. The most famous, of course, is *bolognese*, or *ragù*. The tastiest version boasts not only minced beef, tomato purée, and onions but chopped chicken livers, ham, carrots, celery, white wine, and nutmeg. Other popular sauces are the simple *pomodoro* (tomato, garlic, and basil), *aglio e olio* (garlic, olive oil, and chilli peppers), *carbonara* (chopped bacon and eggs), *matriciana* (salt pork and tomato), *pesto* (basil and garlic ground in olive oil with pine nuts and parmesan cheese), and *vongole* (clams).

Pizza: Another Italian invention familiar around the world, pizza is in reality a much more elaborate affair than you may be used to. Toppings generally include the following ingredients: tomato, ham, anchovies, cheese, mushrooms, peppers, artichoke hearts, egg, clams, tuna fish, garlic—or any other ingredient that takes the cook's fancy. Pizza is especially popular after the opera or theatre.

Meat: Most main courses will be a hearty meat dish. *Vitello* (veal) has pride of place, with the great speciality of Rome, *saltimbocca* (literally "jump in the mouth"), a veal roll with ham, sage, and Marsala wine. Try the *costoletta* (pan-fried cutlet in breadcrumbs), or the *scaloppine al limone* (with lemon). *Osso buco* is a delicious dish of stewed veal shin-bone in butter, with tomatoes, onions, and mushrooms.

Manzo (beef), *maiale* (pork), and *agnello* (lamb) are most often served in straightforward style, charcoal-grilled or *al forno* (roasted). *Bistecca alla fiorentina* (grilled Florentine T-bone) is the emperor of all steaks and costs a royal ransom, but you should try it once. After that, the lesser proportions of the *bistecca* or *filetto* are something of an anticlimax.

Romans also claim the best *capretto* (roast kid), *porchetta* (suckling pig)—roasted whole on a spit—and *abbacchio* (spring lamb), flavoured with garlic, sage, and rosemary, and seasoned just before serving with anchovy paste. The most common chicken dishes are *pollo alla diavola* (grilled) or *petti di pollo alla bolognese* (filleted with ham and cheese).

Fish: Prepared in a simple way—grilled, steamed or fried. You should look out for *spigola* (sea bass), *triglia* (red mullet), *pesce spada* (swordfish), and *coda di rospo* (angler fish). The *fritto misto* is mixed fried seafood, mostly shrimp and octopus.

Vegetables: These are ordered separately, as they do not automatically come with the meat dish. What is available will depend on the season, but you are most likely to find *spinaci* (spinach), *cicoria* (endives), *fagioli* (green beans in butter and garlic), *piselli* (peas), and *zucchini* (courgettes).

Aristocrats among cooked vegetables are the *funghi porcini* (big boletus mushrooms), which sometimes come stuffed (*ripieni*) with bacon, garlic, parsley, and cheese. The white truffle is an autumn delicacy. Try also *peperonata* (red peppers stewed with tomatoes) or *melanzane* (aubergine) stuffed with anchovies, olives, and capers. The Jewish ghetto originated the spectacular *carciofi alla giudea* (whole artichokes, crisply fried — stem, heart, leaves, and all).

Cheeses: The famous *parmigiano* (Parmesan), far better than the exported product, is eaten separately, not just grated over soup or pasta. Try also the blue *gorgonzola*, creamy *fontina*, pungent cow's milk *taleggio,* or ewe's milk *pecorino*. *Ricotta* can be sweetened with sugar and cinnamon for a delicious treat.

Dessert: Usually means *gelati*, the creamiest ice cream in the world. It's usually better in an ice-cream parlour (*gelateria*) than in the average *trattoria*. *Zuppa inglese* (literally "English soup"), the Italian version of trifle, can be anything from an extremely thick and sumptuous mixture of fruit, cream, cake, and Marsala to a disappointing sickly slice of cake. You may prefer the coffee-flavoured trifle or *tirami sù* (literally "pick me up"). *Zabaglione* (whipped egg yolks, sugar, and Marsala) should be served warm or sent back. Fruit can be a succulent alternative: *fragole* (strawberries), served with whipped cream or lemon; *uva* (grapes); and *albicocche* (apricots).

DRINKS

Wine: All restaurants will offer the open wine of the house, red or white, in ¼-litre, ½-litre, or 1-litre carafes, as well as a good selection of bottled vintages.

Rome's "local" wine comes from the surrounding province of Lazio. The whites from the Alban Hills, called Castelli Romani, are light and pleasant and can be sweet or dry. The most famous is Frascati. From farther afield, the Chiantis of Tuscany are available everywhere; as are the velvety Valpolicella from the Veneto and Piedmont's full-bodied Barolo. Look out for the unusual Est! Est! Est! from Montefiascone on Lake Bolsena.

Italian beer: Increasing in popularity but not as strong as north European brands.

Italians will also order mineral water (*acqua minerale*) with their meal. Ask for it fizzy (*gassata*) or still (*naturale*).

Apéritif: Bitters such as Campari and Punt e Mes are refreshing with soda and lemon. For after-dinner drinks, try the anise-flavoured *sambuca* with a *mosca,* (coffee bean; literally a fly) swimming in it, or *grappa,* distilled from grapes.

PRICES

While some restaurants offer fixed-price, three-course meals (*menu turistico* or *prezzo fisso*) which will save money, you'll almost always get better food by ordering individual dishes.

You should be warned that by law all restaurants must now issue a receipt indicating the value added tax (IVA). You may be stopped and fined if unable to show that the tax has been paid. The bill usually includes cover (*coperto*) and service (*servizio*).

To Help You Order...

Do you have a set menu?
I'd like a/an/some...

**Avete un menù a prezzo fisso?
Vorrei...**

beer	**una birra**	pepper	**del pepe**
bread	**del pane**	potatoes	**delle patate**
butter	**del burro**	salad	**un'insalata**
coffee	**un caffè**	salt	**del sale**
cream	**della panna**	soup	**una minestra**
fish	**del pesce**	sugar	**dello zucchero**
fruit	**della frutta**	tea	**un tè**
ice-cream	**un gelato**	(mineral)	**dell'acqua**
meat	**della carne**	water	**(minerale)**
milk	**del latte**	wine	**del vino**

...and Read the Menu

aglio	garlic	**lamponi**	raspberries
agnello	lamb	**maiale**	pork
albicocche	apricots	**manzo**	beef
aragosta	spiny lobster	**mela**	apple
arancia	orange	**melanzane**	aubergine
bistecca	beef steak	**merluzzo**	cod
braciola	chop	**ostriche**	oysters
bue	beef	**pesca**	peach
calamari	squid	**piselli**	peas
carciofi	artichokes	**pollo**	chicken
cavolo	cabbage	**pomodori**	tomatoes
cicoria	endive	**prosciutto**	ham
cipolle	onions	**rognoni**	kidneys
crostacei	shellfish	**tacchino**	turkey
fegato	liver	**uovo**	egg
formaggio	cheese	**uva**	grapes
frutti di mare	seafood	**vitello**	veal
funghi	mushrooms	**vongole**	clams

INDEX

99

HANDY TRAVEL TIPS

An A–Z Summary of Practical Information

Listed after some entries is the appropriate Italian translation, usually in the singular, plus a number of phrases that may come in handy during your stay in Italy.

A

ACCOMMODATION (See also CAMPING on page 104, YOUTH HOSTELS on page 127, and the list of RECOMMENDED HOTELS starting on page 130)

Rome's array of lodgings ranges from the spartan to the palatial. Hotels (*albergo*) are classified in five categories, graded from 1 to 5 stars, based on the amenities and comfort they offer. (The Rome Tourist Board no longer uses the term *pensione* in its classifications; these family-style boarding houses are now graded as hotels.) Some Roman-Catholic institutions also take guests at reasonable rates.

In summer and at Easter, booking ahead is important, but for the rest of the year you can normally find accommodation in your preferred category without difficulty. The Rome Tourist Board (EPT) has up-to-date information at its offices in Via Parigi 5, at Fiumicino Airport, and at Termini railway station. The EPT also has information offices at the (Roma-Nord) Salaria service area on the A1 *autostrada* (motorway) and at the (Roma-Sud) Frascati service area on the A2 *autostrada*. Alternatively, H.R. Hotel Reservation offers a telematic reservation service free of charge (to book, call 066991000) and has desks at Fiumicino airport and Termini railway station.

If you plan to walk to most of Rome's sights, which is usually the best way, choose a hotel in the Centro Storico (historic centre — see page 25). Room rates quoted by all categories of hotels should include taxes and service. Rates for 4- and 5-star hotels are also inclusive of air-conditioning.

Rome has several "daytime" hotels, one of them at Termini station. They provide bathrooms, hairdresser, and left-luggage facilities.

I'd like a single/ double room.	**Vorrei una camera singola/doppia.**
with bath/shower	**con bagno/doccia**
What's the rate per night?	**Qual è il prezzo per notte?**

Rome

AIRPORTS *(aeroporto)*

Rome is served by two airports, Leonardo da Vinci, commonly referred to as **Fiumicino**, 30 km (18 miles) southwest of the city, and **Ciampino**, 15 km (9 miles) southeast of the city on the Via Appia Nuova. Fiumicino handles mainly scheduled air traffic, while Ciampino is used by most charter companies. Fiumicino has two terminals (domestic and international), a 5-minute walk apart.

Fiumicino is connected by train to Termini railway station (service approximately every hour; journey 30 minutes; price L12,000) and Tiburtina railway station (service every 20 minutes via Trastevere, Ostiense stations; journey 40 minutes; price L7,000). A late night bus runs between Fiumicino and Tiburtina station during the hours when there is no train service. Termini is connected to metro lines A and B and buses which can take you all over the city; Tiburtina is linked to the centre by a variety of buses.

Information: Fiumicino, tel. 65951; Ciampino, tel. 794941.

B

BICYCLE and MOTORCYCLE HIRE

You can hire bicycles from several locations, including the entrance to the metro at Piazza di Spagna and the Villa Borghese underground car-park (lower level, third sector) from I Bike Roma; tel. 3225240. A telephone hire service offers delivery at your hotel. Scooters and bicycles can both be hired from Scoot-a-long, Via Cavour 302, tel. 6780206; Collalti, Via dei Pellegrini 82 (near Campo dei Fiori), tel. 68801084; and St. Peter Moto, Via di Porta Castello 43, tel. 6875714/6874909. You have to be over 21 years old to hire a scooter.

C

CAMPING *(campeggio)*

Rome and the surrounding countryside have some 20 official campsites, mostly equipped with electricity, water, and toilet facilities. They are listed in the telephone directory under "Campeggio-Ostelli-

Villaggi Turistici," or contact Roma Camping, Via Aurelia 831; tel. 6623018. You can also contact the Tourist Office for a comprehensive list of sites and rates. The Touring Club Italiano (TCI) and the Automobile Club d'Italia (ACI) publish lists of campsites and tourist villages, available at bookstores or the Tourist Office. You are strongly advised to stick to the official sites.

If you enter Italy with a caravan (trailer), you should be able to show an inventory (with two copies) of the material and equipment in the caravan, e.g., dishes and linen.

Is there a campsite near here?	**C'è un campeggio qui vicino?**
We have a tent/caravan (trailer).	**Abbiamo la tenda/la roulotte**.

CAR HIRE *(autonoleggio)*

The major car-hire firms have offices at the airports as well as in the city; they are listed in the telephone directory. It is possible to rent a car in one Italian city and give it up in another. To rent a car you must be at least 21 years of age and have held a valid driver's licence for at least a year. Mandatory third-party insurance is included in the rates. Note that hiring a car is expensive in Italy. It may be cheaper and more convenient to arrange car hire in advance through your automobile association or a company in your home country, or as part of a fly-drive package.

I'd like to rent a car	**Vorrei noleggiare una macchina**
(tomorrow).	**(per domani)**.
for one day	**per un giorno**
for one week	**per una settimana**

CLIMATE

From mid-June to mid-September, temperatures in Rome range from hot to very hot. Winters are cool, even cold, and at times rainy, with occasional snow — but often you will find the sun does shine. Spring and autumn are pleasantly mild.

Rome

		J	F	M	A	M	J	J	A	S	O	N	D
Max*	°F	52	55	59	66	74	82	87	86	79	71	61	55
	°C	11	13	15	19	23	28	31	30	26	22	16	13
Min*	°F	40	42	45	50	56	63	67	67	62	55	49	44
	°C	4	5	7	10	12	17	19	19	18	13	9	6

*Minimum temperatures are measured just before sunrise, maximum temperatures in the afternoon.

COMPLAINTS *(reclamo)*

In hotels, shops, and restaurants, complaints should be made to the manager (*direttore*) or the proprietor (*proprietario*). If satisfaction is not quickly forthcoming, make clear your intention to report the incident to the Tourist Office (see page 126), or to the police (see page 119) for more serious matters. Arguments over taxi fares can usually be settled by checking the notices in taxis specifying supplementary charges (airport runs, night surcharges, etc.). It is generally advisable to try to reach an agreement over price in advance.

CONSULATES *(consolato)*

Contact the offices of your diplomatic representative if you lose your passport or run into serious trouble. The consulate can also provide lists of doctors, lawyers, and interpreters. These are the main consulate offices for English-speaking visitors:

Australia: Via Alessandria 21/5; tel. 852721.

Canada: Via G.B. de Rossi 27; tel. 445981.

Eire: Largo Nazareno 3; tel. 6782541.

New Zealand: Via Zara 28; tel. 4402928.

South Africa: Via Tanaro 14; tel. 8419794.

U.K.: Via XX Settembre 80/a; tel. 4825441.

U.S.A.: Via Vittorio Veneto 121; tel. 46741.

CRIME

Petty theft is an endless annoyance, but cases of violence against tourists are rare. It's wise to leave any documents you don't need and excess cash in the hotel safe and keep what you take with you, including credit cards, in an inside pocket or a pouch inside your clothes. Handbags are particularly vulnerable, so be attentive on crowded public transport or in secluded streets. Beware of begging children and don't let them distract your attention for a moment; they are very adept pickpockets. (They often linger around Termini train station, posing a serious menace to travelers.) It's a good idea to make photocopies of your tickets, driving licence, passport, and other vital documents to facilitate reporting any theft and obtaining replacements.

If you park your car, lock it and empty it of everything, with the glove compartment open, to discourage prospective thieves. Wherever possible, try to park in a garage or attended parking area.

If you are robbed, report the theft to the police, so that you have a statement to file with your insurance claim. The central police station is at: Questura Centrale, Via San Vitale 15; tel. 4686.

I want to report a theft.	**Voglio denunciare un furto**.
My wallet/handbag/passport/ ticket has been stolen.	**Mi hanno rubato il portafoglio/laborsa/ il passaporto/il biglietto**.

CUSTOMS and ENTRY FORMALITIES

For a stay of up to three months, a valid passport is sufficient for citizens of Australia, Canada, New Zealand, and the United States. Visitors from Eire, the United Kingdom, and other EU countries need only an identity card to enter Italy. Tourists from South Africa must have a visa.

Here are some of the main items you can take into Italy duty-free and, when returning home, back to your own country:

Rome

Into:	Cigarettes		Cigars		Tobacco	Spirits		Wine
Italy [1]	200	or	50	or	250g	2*l*	and	2*l*
Australia	200	or	250g	or	250g	1*l*	or	1*l*
Canada	200	and	50	and	400g	1.1*l*	or	1.1*l*
Eire	200	or	50	or	250g	1*l*	and	2*l*
N. Zealand	200	or	50	or	250g	1.1*l*	and	4.5*l*
S. Africa	400	and	50	and	250g	1*l*	and	2*l*
U.K.	400	or	100	or	500g	1*l*	and	2*l*
U.S.A.	200	and	100	and	[2]	1*l*	or	1*l*
Within the EU [3]	800	and	200	and	1kg	10*l*	and	90*l*

[1] For non-European residents or residents outside the EU or from duty-free shops within EU countries.

[2] a reasonable quantity

[3] Guidelines for non duty-free within the EU. For the import of larger amounts you must be able to prove that the goods are for your own personal use. For EU duty-free allowances see [1] above.

Currency restrictions. As a foreign tourist, you may import unlimited amounts in local or other currencies, but to take more than L20,000,000 or the equivalent in foreign money out again, you must fill in a V2 declaration form at the border when you arrive.

I've nothing to declare. **Non ho nulla da dichiarare**.

It's for my personal use. **Per mio uso personale**.

D

DISABLED VISITORS

Cobblestone streets and steep hills are just two of the problems facing travellers with disabilities visiting Rome. Facilities for the disabled in the city are still thin on the ground, but there are signs that the authorities are beginning to take steps to remedy this. There are lavatories for disabled people at both the main airports, and at Stazione Termini and Piazza San Pietro. St. Peter's and the Vatican Museums are wheelchair-accessible, but unfortunately this is not yet the case with many of the city's other major museums and galleries.

Up-to-date information on access to museums and monuments is provided by the Rome Tourist Board's free leaflet, *Musei e Monumenti di Roma*. The Milan-based Harvey Club (Via Luosi 38, 20131 Milan; tel. 02-2614 1600) arranges tours for disabled people in Italy and also provides information and advice.

DRIVING

Entering Italy. To bring your car into Italy, you will need:
• an international driving licence or valid national one
• car registration papers
• green insurance card (an extension to your regular insurance policy, making it valid specifically for Italy)
• a red warning triangle in case of breakdown
• national identity sticker for your car.

Drivers of cars that are not their own must have the owner's written permission. Before leaving home, check with your automobile association about the latest regulations concerning petrol coupons (these give tourists access to cheaper fuel) in Italy, as these are constantly changing.

Speed limits on the *autostrade* toll highways are 130 km/h (80 mph); on other roads the limit is 90 km/h (55 mph). The limit in built-up areas is generally 60 km/h (37 mph).

Driving conditions. Seat belts are compulsory. Drive on the right, pass on the left. Traffic on major roads has right of way over that entering from side roads, but this is frequently ignored, so be very careful. At intersections of roads of similar importance the car on the right theoretically has the right of way. When passing other vehicles, or remaining in the left-hand (passing) lane, keep your directional indicator flashing.

Motorways are designed for fast and safe driving; a toll is collected for each section. Take a ticket from an automatic machine or from the booth attendant and pay at the other end according to the distance you have travelled.

Driving in Rome. Only the most intrepid motorist stays cool in the face of the Romans' hair-raising driving habits. However, Roman drivers are not reckless — simply attuned to a different concept of driving. If you observe the following ground rules and venture with prudence into the urban traffic whirlpool, you stand a good chance of coming out unscathed.

Glance round to right and left and in your rearview mirror all the time; other drivers are doing the same, and they've developed quick reflexes. Treat traffic lights which are theoretically in your favour and white lines across merging side streets with caution — don't take priority for granted. To make progress in a traffic jam in one of Rome's squares, inch gently but confidently forward into the snarl-up. Waving on another driver, courteously letting him or her cut in ahead of you, is tantamount to abdicating your rights as a motorist.

Most of the city centre between the river, Piazza del Popolo, Piazza di Spagna, and Piazza Venezia is closed to traffic 6:30am-6pm and on Friday and Saturday evenings 10:30pm-1am, except for taxis, buses, and cars with special permits. It is advisable to look for a good parking spot on arrival (see page 111) and then use public transport or taxis.

Traffic police (*polizia stradale*). The traffic police patrol the highways and byways on motorcycles or in Alfa Romeos, usually light blue. Speeding fines often have to be paid on the spot — ask for a receipt (*ricevuta*). All cities and many towns and villages have signs posted at the outskirts indicating the telephone number of the local traffic police or *carabinieri*. The headquarters in Rome are at Viale Romania 45, tel. 80981.

Breakdowns. Call boxes are located at regular intervals on the *autostrade* in case of breakdowns or other emergencies. You can dial 116 for breakdown service from the ACI. Temporary membership in the ACI can be taken out at main frontier posts.

Fuel and oil. Service stations abound in Italy, usually with at least one mechanic on duty. Most stations close on Sundays, and also every day from noon to 3pm, but many have self-service pumps available during closing hours. Stations along the *autostrade* are open 24 hours a day. Fuel (*benzina*) is sold at government-set prices and comes in super (98-100 octane), lead-free (95-octane), normal (86-88-octane), and diesel. Unleaded petrol is now also common. Look for the pumps with green labels marked *senza piombo* (without lead) or the abbreviation SP.

Fluid measures

Distance

Parking (See also CRIME on page 107). For motorized tourists as well as residents, parking is one of Rome's greatest challenges. Your wisest course is to find a legal parking place for the duration of your stay and see the city on foot or by public transport. If you park in a tow-away zone, you may have to pay a heavy fine and spend many hours getting your car released. If your car is towed away, contact the *vigili urbani* (municipal police) central headquarters at Via Consolazione 4 (tel. 67691). The Rome Automobile Club (ACI) has various car parks in the centre, e.g., Piazza del Popolo, Via Barberini. There are also private car parks e.g. Parking Ludovisi (tel. 4740692) at Via Ludovisi, open 5:30am-1:30am; or at Villa Borghese (always open).

Road signs. Most road signs employed in Italy are the international pictographs, but here are some written ones you may come across:

Accendere le luci	Use headlights
Deviazione	Diversion (Detour)
Divieto di sorpasso	No overtaking (passing)
Divieto di sosta	No stopping
Lavori in corso	Roadwork
Passaggio a livello	Level crossing
Pericolo	Danger
Rallentare	Slow down
Senso unico	One-way street
Senso vietato/Vietato l'inresso	No entry
Zona pedonale	Pedestrian zone
driving licence	**patente**

car registration papers	**libretto di circolazione**
green card	**carta verde**
Where's the nearest car park?	**Dov'è il parcheggio più vicino?**
Can I park here?	**Posso parcheggiare qui?**
Are we on the right road for...?	**Siamo sulla strada giusta per...?**
Fill the tank, please.	**Per favore, faccia il pieno.**
super/normal	**super/normale**
unleaded	**senza piombo**
diesel	**gasolio**
Check the oil/tyres/ battery.	**Controlli l'olio/i pneumatici/la batteria.**
I've had a breakdown.	**Ho avuto un guasto.**
There's been an accident.	**C'è stato un incidente.**

E

ELECTRIC CURRENT

Electric current is 220 volts, 50 Hz AC. Bring a multiple adapter plug (*una presa multipla*), or buy one as required.

EMERGENCIES

In an emergency you can phone the following numbers all over Italy 24 hours a day:

Emergency services (ambulance, fire, police): **113**
Carabinieri (for urgent police action): **112**
Fire: **115**
Road assistance (ACI): **116**

Here are some further useful phrases that we hope you won't need to employ:

Careful!	**Attenzione!**
Fire!	**Incendio!**

Help!	**Aiuto!**
Stop thief!	**Al ladro!**

ETIQUETTE

On entering and leaving a shop, restaurant, or office, the expected greeting is *buon giorno* (good morning) or *buona sera* (good evening). When approaching anyone with an enquiry, the correct form is *per favore* (please), and for any service say *grazie* (thanks), to which the reply is *prego* (don't mention it/you're welcome).

Introductions are usually accompanied by handshaking and the phrase *piacere* (it's a pleasure). With people you know well, *ciao* is the casual form of greeting or farewell. *Salve* is a casual form of farewell less intimate than *ciao*. When wished *buon appetito* before a meal, reply *grazie, altrettanto* (thank you, and the same to you).

How are you?	**Come sta?**
Very well, thanks.	**Molto bene, grazie.**

G

GETTING TO ROME

If the choice of ways to go is bewildering, the complexity of fares and regulations can be downright stupefying. A reliable travel agent will have full details of all the latest flight possibilities, fares, and regulations.

By Air: Rome's Fiumicino (Leonardo da Vinci) Airport is on inter-continental air routes and is linked by frequent services to cities in Europe, North America, the Middle East, and Africa. Average flying times are: New York–Rome 8 hours; Los Angeles–Rome 15 hours; London–Rome 2½ hours; Sydney–Rome 26 hours.

By Car: Cross-Channel car ferries link the U.K. with France, Belgium, and Holland. Once on the continent, you can put your car on a train to Milan (starting points include Boulogne, Paris, and Cologne). Alternatively, you can drive from the Channel coast to Rome without leaving a motorway. The main north-south (Milan–Florence–Reggio di Calabria) and east-west (L'Aquila–Civitavecchia) motorways connect with Rome via a huge ring motorway (*grande raccordo anulare*).

Rome

By Rail: InterRail cards are valid in Italy, as is the **Eurailpass** for non-European residents (sign up before you leave home). Within Italy, you can obtain an **Italian Tourist Ticket** (*Biglietto Turistico di Libera Circolazione*) for unlimited first- or second-class rail travel for 8, 15, 21, or 30 days.

The **Freedom Pass** offers travel on any 3, 5, or 10 days within one month in several European countries. Contact the International Rail Centre, Victoria Station, London SW1Y 1JY (tel. 0171 834 2345).

The **Kilometric Ticket** (*Biglietto Chilometrico*) can be used by up to five people and is valid for 20 trips or 3,000 km (1,860 miles), first or second class, over a period of two months.

GUIDES and TOURS

Most hotels in Rome can arrange for multilingual guides or interpreters. At some museums and sites, taped tour commentaries can be rented. The Italian Tourist Agency, CIT, Piazza della Repubblica 68 (tel. 47941), and many private firms offer tours of all the major sites, plus excursions to other points of interest. Often tourists are picked up and dropped off at their hotels.

ATAC, Rome's municipal bus company, provides an inexpensive 3-hour sightseeing tour which takes in many of the major sites. Tours on ATAC bus 110 depart at 2:30pm from Piazza dei Cinquecento (tel. 46952252); tickets are available from the ATAC information booth in the square. Another cheap tour round the historic centre is by local minibus no. 119, starting from Piazza Augusto Imperatore.

L

LAUNDRY and DRY-CLEANING

Most hotels handle laundry and dry-cleaning. Naturally it is cheaper to do your own washing (or leave it with the attendant) at a *lavanderia* or hand it in at a *tintoria*, which usually offers a normal or express service.

When will it be ready?	**Quando sarà pronto?**
I must have this for tomorrow morning.	**Mi serve per domani mattina.**

LOST PROPERTY

Cynics believe that anything lost in Italy is lost forever, but that's not necessarily true in Rome. Restaurants will more often than not have the "lost" briefcase, guidebook, or camera waiting for you at the cashier's desk. If you're not sure where the loss occurred, have your hotel receptionist call the lost property office (*ufficio oggetti rinvenuti* or *smarriti*). Report lost documents to the police (see page 119) or your consulate (see page 106).

Rome's general lost property office is the Ufficio Oggetti Rinvenuti at Via Bettoni 1; tel. 5816040. There are lost property offices at the Termini railway station (tel. 47301) and at ATAC in Via Bettoni 1; tel. 5816040. For losses on the metro call 5753 3620.

I've lost my passport/ wallet/handbag.	**Ho perso il passaporto/ portafoglio/la borsetta.**

MAPS *(pianta)*

The offices of the Rome Tourist Board give away basic street plans featuring a selection of local information. More detailed maps are on sale at newsstands. A useful bus network map is sold at the ATAC information booth in Piazza dei Cinquecento (near Termini Station).

MEDICAL CARE

If your health insurance policy does not cover you while abroad, take out a short-term policy before leaving home. Visitors from EU countries carrying the E111 form available from their local post office are entitled to emergency medical and hospital treatment under the Italian social security system. The E111 form explains the steps you will need to take to obtain treatment in Italy.

If you need medical care, ask your hotel receptionist to help you find a doctor (or dentist) who speaks English. Both the U.S. and British consulates (see page 106) have lists of English-speaking doctors. Local Health Units of the Italian National Health Service are listed in the phone directory under *Unità Sanitaria Locale*. The first-aid (*pronto soccorso*) section of hospitals handles medical emergencies.

Rome

Pharmacies. The Italian *farmacia* is open during shopping hours (see OPENING HOURS on page 117). Usually one operates at night and at weekends for each district on a rotating basis. Some are open 24 hrs, e.g., Farmacia Grieco (Piazza della Repubblica 67). The opening schedule for duty pharmacies is posted on every pharmacy door and in the local newspapers. We advise you to bring along with you an adequate supply of any prescribed medication, particularly since new laws have made prescriptions mandatory for many medicines.

I need a doctor/a dentist.	**Ho bisogno di un medico/dentista.**
Where's the nearest (all-night) chemist?	**Dov'è la farmacia (di turno) più vicina?**

MONEY MATTERS (See also OPENING HOURS on page 117)

Currency. Italy's monetary unit is the *lira* (plural *lire*, abbreviated L or Lit).

Coins: L10, 20, 50, 100, 200, 500.
Notes: L1,000, 2,000, 5,000, 10,000, 50,000, 100,000.

For currency restrictions, see CUSTOMS AND ENTRY FORMALITIES on p.107.

Currency exchange. Currency exchange offices (*cambio*) are usually open from 9am to 1:30pm and 2:30 to 6pm. Many are closed on Saturday. Exchange rates here are less advantageous than those offered by banks. A flat rate of commission is common, so it is not worth changing small amounts frequently. Passports are sometimes required when changing money. It is worth noting that many banks now operate automatic currency-exchange machines and you may be able to use your cash card at some cash points.

Credit cards and traveller's cheques. Most hotels, shops, and restaurants take credit cards. Traveller's cheques are accepted almost everywhere, but you will get better value if you exchange your cheques for lire at a bank or *cambio*. Passports are required when cashing cheques. Eurocheques are fairly easily cashed in Italy.

I want to change some pounds/dollars.	**Desidero cambiare delle sterline/dei dollari.**

| Do you accept traveller's cheques? | **Accetta traveller's cheques?** |
| Can I pay with this credit card? | **Posso pagare con la carta di credito?** |

NEWSPAPERS and MAGAZINES

A good selection of British and international English-language newspapers and magazines are on sale, sometimes a day late, at the airport and main railway station, and at news-stands in the city centre. Prices are high for all foreign publications.

The supplement *Trovaroma*, published in the Thursday edition of the newspaper *La Repubblica*, provides comprehensive listings of cultural events in Rome. The monthly *Carnet di Roma*, published by the Rome Tourist Board in Italian, English, French, and German, also lists events, as does the fortnightly English-language publication *Wanted in Rome*, available in Rome's English bookshops.

| Have you any English-language newspapers? | **Aveti giornali in inglese?** |

OPENING HOURS

Even within Rome, opening hours vary. In true Mediterranean fashion, much of the city shuts or slows down after lunch. However, for some offices the modern non-stop business day is gradually creeping in. The following is therefore just a guideline.

Shops. Open 9am to 1pm and 4 to 8pm (summer) and until 7:30pm (winter), Monday to Saturday (half-day closing is usually Monday morning); however, some shops in the centre open 10am-7pm and department stores are open all day. Food stores open 7am to 1:30pm and 4 to 7:30pm in the winter and 8pm in the summer (half-day closing usually Thursday afternoon, though not for supermarkets). Tourist resort shops stay open all day, every day, in high season.

Rome

Post offices. Normally open 8:30am to 5:30pm, Monday to Friday, until noon on Saturday. The main post office in Piazza San Silvestro stays open until 9pm. Closed on Sundays.

Banks. 8:30am to 1:30pm and again for an hour or so in the afternoon (usually 3-4pm), Monday to Friday.

Principal businesses. Most large businesses 9am to 5 or 6pm Monday-Friday; smaller businesses 8:30 or 9am to 1 or 1:30pm and 3:30 or 4 to 6 or 7pm, Monday to Friday (sometimes Saturday morning).

Pharmacies. 8:30am to 1pm and 4 to 8pm (though 24 hrs for some).

Churches are generally open from early morning to 12 or 12:30pm, and from 4 or 5 to 7pm. St. Peter's and some of the larger basilicas remain open all day.

Museums and historic sites. These are usually open Tuesday to Sunday, from 9am to 2pm (if not earlier), and, in some cases, also from 5 to 8pm. Check with tourist booths, the *Trovaroma* supplement of *La Repubblica*, or *Roma C'è* (see page 117).

The following attractions are open on Monday: Vatican museum, closed Sunday (except last Sunday in August when entrance is free); Castel Sant'Angelo open every morning, Monday and Thursday till 6pm; Keats-Shelley Memorial house, open weekdays; Catacombs of St. Calixtus, closed Wednesday; Catacombs of St. Sebastian, closed Thursday; Colosseum, closed Wednesday and Saturday.

PLANNING YOUR BUDGET

To give you an idea of what to expect, here's a list of average prices in *lire* (L). However, remember that all prices must be regarded as approximate.

Airport transfer. Train from Fiumicino Airport to Roma Termini railway station L12,000, and to Tiburtina railway station L7,000. Bus from Ciampino Airport to Anagnina Metro station L1,000. Taxi from Fiumicino to city centre L50,000-60,000.

Baby-sitters. L12,000 per hour; transport and agency fee are usually included in the price.

Buses, metro, and trains (urban network). Standard fare (*Biglietto integrato a tempo*) L1,500 (valid for 75 minutes); day ticket (*biglietto integrato giornaliero*) L6,000; weekly ticket (*carta integrato settimanale*) L20,000.

Camping. L8,000 per person per night, caravan (trailer) or camper L8,000, tent L5,000, car L4,000, motorbike L2,000.

Car hire. Fiat Panda 45 L120,000 per day with unlimited mileage, L550,000 per week with unlimited mileage. Alfa 33 L170,000 per day with unlimited mileage, L750,000 per week with unlimited mileage.

Cigarettes (packet of 20). Italian brands L3,300 and up, imported brands L4,800.

Entertainment. Cinema L10,000, discotheque (entry and first drink) L20,000-30,000, outdoor opera L30,000-90,000.

Hairdressers. Woman's shampoo and set or blow dry L30,000-50,000, permanent wave L100,000-120,000. Man's haircut L15,000-25,000, with shampoo L20,000-40,000.

Hotels (double room with bath, including tax and service). 5-star L500,000-650,000, 4-star L260,000-500,000, 3-star L140,000-260,000, 2-star L90,000-140,000, 1-star L50,000-90,000.

Meals and drinks. Continental breakfast L5,000, lunch/dinner in fairly good establishment L35,000-50,000, coffee served at a table L3,000-5,000, served at the bar L900-1,500, bottle of beer L3,000-6,000, soft drinks L1,500-3,000, aperitif L5,000 and up.

Museums. L2,500-12,000; Vatican Museums L13,000.

Shopping bag. 500g of bread L1,000 and up, 250g of butter L2,500 and up, 6 eggs L1,200 and up, 500g of beefsteak L11,000, 200g of coffee L3,000 and up, bottle of wine L3,500 and up.

Taxis. Minimum charge L6,400 for the first 9 minutes or 3km (1.8 miles), L300 for each successive 45 seconds. Surcharge for nighttime, holidays, and each piece of luggage L1,000-3,000.

POLICE

The municipal police (*vigili urbani*), dressed in navy blue or summer white uniforms with white helmets, handle city traffic and other city police tasks. They are courteous and helpful to tourists, though they rarely speak a foreign language. Those who do act as interpreters display a special badge on their uniforms, which indicates the languages they speak.

The *carabinieri*, dressed in dark blue uniforms with a red stripe down the side of the trousers, deal with theft, more serious crimes, demonstrations, and military affairs. The national, or state, police (*polizia di stato*) are distinguished by their navy blue jackets and light blue trousers, and handle other police and administrative matters. (For traffic police details see also DRIVING on page 109). The all-purpose emergency number, **113**, will get you police assistance.

Where's the nearest police station?	**Dov'è il più vicino posto di polizia?**

POST OFFICES *(posta or ufficio postale)*

Post offices handle telegrams, mail, and money transfers. Look for the yellow sign with PT in black. Postage stamps are also sold at tobacconists and at some hotel desks. Post boxes are red; the slot marked *Per la Città* is for local mail only; the one labelled *Altre Destinazioni* is for all other destinations. Post to and from Rome can be slow. The Vatican post is more efficient; buy Vatican stamps near the Tourist Office in St. Peter's Square and use the post boxes there.

For a short stay it is not worth arranging to receive mail. However, there is a *poste restante* service at the main post office in Piazza San Silvestro. Don't forget your passport for identification when you go to pick up mail. You will have to pay a small fee.

Telegrams (*telegramme*) can be sent to destinations inside and outside Italy, as can telex messages. There is now a rapidly growing facsimile service.

PUBLIC HOLIDAYS *(festa)*

Banks, government offices, and most shops and museums close on public holidays. When one falls on a Thursday or a Tuesday, Italians may make a *ponte* (bridge) to the weekend, meaning that Friday or Monday is taken off as well.

1 January	*Capodanno*	New Year's Day
6 January	*Epifania*	Epiphany

25 April	*Festa della Liberazione*	Liberation Day
1 May	*Primo Maggio*	May Day
15 August	*Ferragosto*	Assumption Day
1 November	*Ognissanti*	All Saints' Day
8 December	*L'Immacolata Concezione*	Immaculate Conception
25 December	*Natale*	Christmas Day
26 December	*Santo Stefano*	St. Stephen's Day
Moveable date:	*Lunedi di Pasqua*	Easter Monday

In addition, Rome has a local holiday on 29 June, the *Festa di San Pietro e San Paolo*, the Feast of Saints Peter and Paul, the city's patron saints, when everything closes. Get to St. Peter's Square early if you want to be a part of this as there are huge crowds.

PUBLIC TRANSPORT (See also TAXIS on page 124)

Underground/Subway (*metropolitana* or *metrò*). Rome has two underground railway lines. Line A runs from Via Ottaviano near the Vatican southeast to Via Anagnina, stopping at more than 20 stations and passing close to many of Rome's popular tourist sights. The intersecting Line B runs from Rebibbia in the northeastern part of the city through Stazione Termini to EUR in the southwest. Some trains branch off at Magliana and go on to the coast, reaching Ostia Antica and Lido di Ostia. Metro stations are identified by a large red sign containing a white letter M. Tickets are sold at newsstands and tobacconists, or can be purchased from machines at the stations.

Buses (*autobus*). Rome's fleet of orange buses serves every corner of the city. Although crowded on certain routes and at rush hours, they are an inexpensive way of crossing the city. Each bus stop (*fermata*) indicates the buses stopping there, their routes, and frequency. Tickets for buses must be bought in advance from ATAC booths, some newsstands and tobacconists, or automatic dispensers. Enter by the rear doors and punch your ticket in a machine; exit by the middle doors. A single ticket is valid for 75 minutes and can be used on as many buses as you like but only once on the metro or train. Daily tickets (BIG) let you travel as much as you like by train, bus, and metro. Weekly tickets (CIG) are sold at the ATAC (transport authority) information booth in Piazza dei Cinquecento, in front of Stazione Termini. Network maps are available from the ATAC booth and from newsstands. COTRAL (tel. 5915551) operates bus services to the outskirts of Rome. Buses to the Roman hills (e.g., Albano, Frascati, Castelgandolfo) leave from Anagnina metro station.

Horse cabs (*carrozzelle*). A familiar sight in Rome for centuries, horse-drawn carriages now number only a few dozen. They can be found at many of the major tourist sites across the city, including St. Peter's Square, the Spanish Steps, and the Colosseum. A complete tour around the centre of the city will cost you around L150,000.

Trains. The Italian State Railways (*Ferrovie dello Stato* — FS) operate an extensive network all over the country. Although fares have been rising in recent years, they are still among the lowest in Europe. Choose your train carefully, as journey times (and ticket prices) vary a good deal. The following list describes the various types of train:

Eurocity (*EC*); international express, first class only, reservation and surcharge.

Intercity (*IC*)/*Rapido*; high-speed express, first and second class, reservation, and surcharge.

Espresso (*EXPR*); long-distance trains stopping at main stations.

Diretto (*DIR*); slower than the Espresso, makes local stops.

Locale (*L*); local train which stops at almost every station.

Metropolitana (*servizi dedicati*); connecting service from airports and cities to major cities.

Children under the age of 12 travel half price; those under the age of 4 years (not occupying a seat) travel free.

Tickets can be purchased and reservations made at a local travel agency or at the railway station. Better-class trains have dining-service or self-service cars which offer refreshments at reasonable prices. If you don't have a reservation, you should arrive at the station at least 20 minutes before departure; Italy's trains are often crowded.

Where's the nearest bus stop/ underground station?	**Dov'è la fermata d'autobus/la stazione della metropolitana più vicina?**
When's the next bus/train to...?	**Quando parte il prossimo autobus/treno per...?**
I'd like a ticket to	**Vorrei un biglietto per...**
single (one-way)	**andata**
return (round-trip)	**andata e ritorno**

R

RADIO AND TV *(radio, televisione)*

The RAI, Italy's state broadcasting system, has three TV channels. There are also various private national and local channels. CBS news from the previous evening is broadcast each morning at 7am Tuesday-Saturday on Telemontecarlo. During the tourist season, RAI radio broadcasts news in English at 10am Monday-Saturday and at 9:30am on Sunday. Vatican Radio carries foreign-language religious news programmes. British (BBC), American (VOA), and Canadian (CBC) stations are easily obtained on short-wave transistor radios.

RELIGION

Roman Catholic mass is celebrated daily and several times on Sunday in Italian. A few churches have occasional services in English. Confessions are heard in English in St. Peter's, Santa Maria Maggiore, St. John Lateran, St. Paul's Outside the Walls, among others.

A number of non-Catholic denominations have congregations in Rome with services in English, including Anglican at All Saints, Via del Babuino 153; American Episcopal at St. Paul's, Via Napoli 58; Scottish Presbyterian at St. Andrew's, Via XX Settembre 7; Methodist at Via Banco di S. Spirito 3. The Jewish Synagogue is at Lungotevere Cenci 9. The city's first mosque is in Via della Moschea.

T

TAXIS (*tassì or taxi*)

Rome's licensed yellow and white taxis may be picked up at a taxi rank (on all the major piazzas) or summoned by telephone. When you phone for a taxi, you pay a surcharge. Extra fees are also charged for luggage, night, holiday, or airport trips: the rates are posted in four languages inside all taxis. A tip of at least 10 percent is customary. Beware of the nonmetred unlicensed taxis (*abusivi*), which charge much more than the normal taxi rates for trips in private cars.

TELEPHONES (*telefono*)

Public telephone booths are scattered at strategic locations throughout the city. Calls can also be made from bars and cafés, indicated by a yellow telephone sign showing a telephone dial and receiver. The main public telephone office, in the Palazzo delle Poste in Piazza San Silvestro, is open day and night.

Older types of public payphones require tokens (*gettoni*) with a value of L200 (available at bars, hotels, post offices, and tobacconists); modern ones, with three slots, take tokens and 100, 200, and 500-lire coins.

From telephones labelled *Teleselezione* you can make direct international calls, but be sure to have a good supply of coins or tokens. Some telephones will take phone cards (*scheda telefonica*) to the value of 5,000 or 10,000 lire, available from some bars, tobacconists, Telecom Italia branches, post offices, and automatic dispensers. If you make a long-distance call from a hotel, expect to be surcharged.

To make a call from a pay phone, insert the token or coin and lift the receiver. The normal dialling tone is a series of long dash sounds. A dot-dot-dot series means the central computer is overloaded; hang up and try again.

The English-speaking operators of the ACI's telephone assistance service provide tourists with information and advice. Dial **116**.

Some useful numbers:

Local directory and other Italian enquiries: **12**
European international operator: **15**
International enquiries: **176**

Intercontinental operator: **170**
Intercontinental enquiries: **1790**
Direct dialling for Australia: 0061, Canada: 001, Eire: 00353, South Africa: 0027, U.K.: 0044, U.S.A.: 001.

Give me ... tokens/L5,000	**Per, favore, mi dia...gettoni/**
(L10,000) phone card please.	**una scheda telefonica.**
	cinquemila (diecimila) lire.
Can you get me this	**Può passarmi questo**
number in...?	**numero a....?**
I'd like a stamp for this letter/	**Desidero un franco-postcard.**
	bollo per questa
	lettera/cartolina.

TIME DIFFERENCES

Italy follows Central European Time (GMT + 1). From the last Sunday in March to the last Sunday in September, clocks are put ahead one hour (GMT + 2).

Summer Time Chart:

New York	London	**Italy**	Jo'burg	Sydney
6am	11am	**noon**	noon	8pm

TIPPING

Though a service charge is added to most restaurant bills, it is customary to leave an additional tip. It is also in order to hand porters, doormen, garage attendants, etc., a little something for their services.

Hotel porter, per bag	L1,500
Hotel maid, per day	L2,000 to L5,000
Lavatory attendant	L1000 or L2000
Waiter	5-10 percent
Taxi driver	10-15 percent
Hairdresser/barber	up to 15 percent
Tour guide	10 percent

TOILETS

Most museums and art galleries have public toilets. Bars, restaurants, cafés, large stores, airports, railway stations, and car parks all have facilities. It is wise to carry your own tissues.

Toilets may be labelled with a symbol of a man or a woman or the initials W.C. Sometimes it will be in Italian, but beware: *Uomini* is for men, *Donne* for women. Equally, *Signori* with a final "i" is for men, but *Signore* with a final "e" means women.

TOURIST INFORMATION

The Italian National Tourist Office (*Ente Nazionale Italiano per il Turismo*, abbreviated ENIT) is represented in Italy and abroad. They publish detailed brochures with up-to-date information on accommodation, means of transport, general tips, and useful addresses.

Australia and New Zealand: c/o Italian Government Tourist Office, Lions Building, 1-1-2 Moto Akasaka, Minato Ku, Tokyo 107; tel. (03) 3478 2051.

Canada: Italian Government Travel Office, Suite 1914, 1 Place Ville-Marie, Montreal, Quebec, H3B 3M9; tel. (514) 866 7667.

Eire: Italian State Tourist Office, 47 Merrion Square, Dublin 2; tel. (01) 766 397.

South Africa: Italian State Tourist Office, P.O. Box 6507, Johannesburg 2000.

United Kingdom: Italian State Tourist Office, 1 Princes Street, London W1R 6AY; tel. (0171) 408 1254.

U.S.A.: Italian Government Travel Office, Suite 1565, 630 Fifth Ave, New York, NY 10111, tel. (212) 245 4822; Italian Government Travel Office, Suite 1046, 401 North Michigan Ave, Suite 3030, Chicago, IL 60611, tel. (312) 644 0996; Italian Government Travel Office, Suite 550, 12400 Wilshire Blvd, Los Angeles CA 90025, tel. (310) 820 0098.

The Tourist Office headquarters in **Rome** are at Via Parigi 11; tel. 488 1851 and Via Parigi 5 (Tourist Assistance), tel. 488 3748, with branches at Stazione Termini and Fiumicino Airport. There are also various tourist booths in the city, e.g., at Largo Goldoni; tel. 6875027.

Where's the tourist office?   **Dov'è l'ufficio turistico?**

WATER

Rome's drinking water, not least from its outdoor fountains, is famous for its flavour and is perfectly safe. Nonetheless, with meals it is customary to drink bottled mineral water. If tap water is not drinkable it will usually carry a sign saying *acqua non potabile.*

I'd like a bottle of mineral water.	**Vorrei una bottiglia di acqua minerale.**
carbonated/still	**gassata/naturale**

WEIGHTS AND MEASURES

(For fluid and distance measures, see DRIVING on p.109.)

Weight

grams	0	100	200	300	400	500	600	700	800	900	1kg
ounces	0	4	8	12	1lb	20	24	28		2lb	

Temperature

°C	-30	-25	-20	-15	-10	-5	0	5	10	15	20	25	30	35	40	45
°F	-20	-10	0	10	20	30	40	50	60	70	80	90	100	110		

Length

cm	0	5	10	15	20	25	30
inches	0	2	4	6	8	10	12

metres	0	1m	2m
ft./yd.	0	1ft.	1yd.	2yd.

YOUTH HOSTELS *(ostello della gioventù)*

Youth hostels are open to holders of membership cards issued by the International Youth Hostels Federation, or by the AIG

Rome

(Associazione Italiana Alberghi per la Gioventù), the Italian Youth Hostels Association, at: Via Cavour 44, 00184 Rome; tel. (06) 4871152; fax 4880492. Open Monday to Thursday 8am-5pm, Friday 8am-3pm.

SOME USEFUL WORDS (see also the cover of this guide for further useful expressions)

Italians appreciate foreigners making an effort to speak their language, even if it's only a few words. In the major hotels and shops, staff usually speak some English.

Bear in mind the following tips on pronunciation:

- "c" is pronounced like ch in change when it is followed by an "e" or an "i."
- "ch" together sounds like the "c" in cat.
- "g" followed by an "e" or an "i" is pronounced like "j" in jet.
- "gh" together sounds like the "g" in gap.
- "gl" together sounds like the "lli" in million.
- "gn" is pronounced like "ni" in onion.
- "sc"+ "i"'s pronounced like "she."

The Berlitz ITALIAN PHRASE BOOK AND DICTIONARY covers all the situations you are likely to encounter in Italy; also useful is the Italian-English/English-Italian pocket dictionary, complete with a menu-reader supplement.

where/when/how	**dove/quando/como**
yesterday/today/tomorrow	**ieri/oggi/domani**
day/week/month/year	**giorno/settimana/mese/anno**
left/right	**sinistra/destra**
up/down	**su/giù**
good/bad	**buono/cattivo**
big/small	**grande/piccolo**
cheap/expensive	**buon mercato/caro**
hot/cold	**caldo/freddo**
open/closed	**aperto/chiuso**
free (vacant)/occupied	**liberto/occupato**
near/far	**vicino/lontano**
early/late	**presto/tardi**
right/wrong	**guisto/sbagliato**

A SELECTION OF HOTELS AND RESTAURANTS

Recommended Hotels

If you are travelling independently you might like to try one of the following hotels recommended by Berlitz. Italian hotels are classified by the government from five stars down to one star according to the facilities they offer. However, the star rating does not give a guide to the character or location of the hotel. As prices do not always include breakfast we recommend that you check this when you book. As a basic guide we have used the symbols below to indicate prices for a double room with bath or shower, including service charge, tax, and VAT:

✪	below L180,000
✪✪	L180,000-300,000
✪✪✪	above L300,000

Aldrovandi Palace *(Parioli)* ✪✪✪ *Via Ulisse Aldrovandi, 15, 00197; Tel. 3223993; fax 3221435.* Hotel with Old World style and service. Many amenities at guests' disposal, including pool, garden, and the Relais La Piscine restaurant. 143 rooms.

Arenula *(Ghetto)* ✪ *Via Santa Maria dei Calderai 47, 00186; Tel. 6879454; fax 6896188.* A comfortable and reasonably priced cheap hotel in the heart of the ghetto. 50 rooms.

Atlante Star *(near St. Peter's)* ✪✪✪ *Via Vitelleschi 34, 00193; Tel. 6879558/6873233; fax 6872300.* Among the attractions offered by this modern hotel is the spectacular view of St. Peter's from its roof-garden restaurant, Les Etoiles. 61 rooms.

Barrett *(near Largo Argentina)* ✪ *Largo Torre Argentina 47, 00186; Tel. 6868481; fax 6892971.* Though extremely small, with only 15 rooms available, this hotel is very central and comfortable and remarkably good value for money.

Brittania *(near Termini Station)* ✪✪ *Via Napoli 64, 00184; Tel. 4883153; fax 4882343.* Comfortable hotel with plenty of amenities such as television, mini-bar, room safe, and hair dryer all included in the very moderate price. 32 rooms.

Campo De' Fiori *(near Campo dei Fiori)* ✪ *Via del Biscione 6, 00186; Tel. 688068865; fax 6876003.* Cheap hotel in Rome's historic centre with good views from the rooftop terrace. 27 rooms.

Carriage *(Corso/Piazza di Spagna)* ✪✪ *Via delle Carrozze 36, 00187; Tel. 6793312; fax 6788279.* Quiet hotel near the Spanish Steps with 27 well-furnished rooms.

Cavalieri Hilton *(Monte Mario)* ✪✪✪ *Via A. Cadlolo 101, 00136; Tel. 35091; fax 35092241.* A peaceful location away from the centre with splendid views from Monte Mario. Outdoor swimming pool, terrace, park, tennis. Outdoor dining. 359 rooms.

Cesari *(near Corso)* ✪ *Via di Pietra 89/a, 00186; Tel. 6792386; fax 6790882.* Pleasant 18th-century hotel with Stendhal, Mazzini, and Garibaldi among its past visitors. 51 rooms.

Columbus *(near St. Peter's)* ✪✪ *Via della Conciliazione 33, 00193; Tel. 6865435; fax 6864874.* Tastefully furnished hotel in a 15th-century palace built by Cardinal Domenico della Rovere. Original frescoes in the lobby. Close to the Vatican, and popular with visiting cardinals. 105 rooms.

Colosseum *(near Santa Maria Maggiore)* ✪ *Via Sforza 10, 00184; Tel. 4827312; fax 4827285.* Comfortable hotel near the Forum and the Colosseum. 45 rooms.

Condotti *(Corso/Piazza di Spagna)* ✪✪ *Via Mario dei Fiori 37, 00187; Tel. 6794661; fax 6790457.* Quiet and comfortable hotel in the heart of the shopping district. 16 rooms.

Rome

Dei Borgognoni *(Corso/Via del Tritone)* ✪✪✪ *Via del Bufalo 126, 00187; Tel. 69941505; fax 69941501.* Elegant hotel offering excellent service. Some of the 50 rooms have a private garden or terrace.

Eden *(near Via Veneto)* ✪✪✪ *Via Ludovisi 49, 00187; Tel. 478121; fax 4821584.* Old-fashioned luxury hotel with good views of the city from the rooftop terrace restaurant. 103 rooms.

Edera *(near Colosseum)* ✪✪ *Via Poliziano 75, 00184; Tel. 70453888/70453946; fax 70453769.* Quiet hotel with garden. No restaurant. 53 rooms.

Erdarelli *(Piazza di Spagna/Largo del Tritone)* ✪ *Via Due Macelli 28, 00187; Tel. 6791265/6784010; fax 6790705.* Unpretentious hotel in a very convenient location not far away from the Spanish Steps. 28 comfortable rooms.

Excelsior ✪✪✪ *Via Veneto 125, 00187; Tel. 47081; fax 4826205.* Grand turn-of-the-century hotel, recently renovated and extremely comfortable. 329 rooms.

Fontana *(near Trevi Fountain)* ✪ *Piazza di Trevi 96, 00187; Tel. 6786113/6790024.* Comfortable hotel housed in a converted monastery overlooking the Trevi Fountain. Roof garden. 27 rooms.

Forum *(near Piazza Venezia)* ✪✪✪ *Via Tor dei Conti 25, 00184; Tel. 6792446; fax 6786479.* Comfortable, elegantly furnished hotel with a spectacular view of the Imperial Forums from its delightful roof-garden restaurant. 81 rooms.

Gerber *(Prati)* ✪ *Via degli Scipioni 241, 00192; Tel. 3216485; fax 3217048.* Small hotel in a quiet neighbourhood. A garden and sun terrace add to the comforts provided. 27 rooms.

Le Grand Hotel *(near Termini Station)* ✪✪✪ *Via Vittorio Emanuele Orlando 3, 00185; Tel. 47091; fax 4747307.* Sophisticated and well-established hotel with ornate decor and monumentally proportioned rooms and salons. 171 rooms.

Gregoriana *(above the Spanish Steps)* ✪✪ *Via Gregoriana 18, 00187; Tel. 6794269; fax 6784258.* A converted convent in a particularly pleasant location. Distinctive Art-Deco style and pretty, comfortable rooms. 19 rooms.

Hassler Villa Medici *(above the Spanish Steps)* ✪✪✪ *Piazza Trinità dei Monti 6, 00187; Tel. 6993401, Reservations 69941607; fax 6789991.* Wonderful location right above the Spanish Steps, with furnishings, service, and a spectacular Roman rooftop view to match. 101 rooms.

Holiday Inn Crowne Plaza Minerva *(Corso/Piazza Navona)* ✪✪✪ *Piazza della Minerva 69, 00186; Tel. 69941888; fax 6794165.* A 17th-century *palazzo* that has been a lodging place since Napoleonic times, and is now Rome's newest luxury hotel. 134 rooms.

D'Inghilterra *(Corso/Piazza di Spagna)* ✪✪✪ *Via Bocca di Leone 21, 00187; Tel. 69981; fax 69922243.* An elegant hotel near the Spanish Steps. Antique furniture and a fine collection of Neapolitan gouaches preserve a distinct flavour of the past. Notable among former celebrity guests here are the writers Ernest Hemingway, Mark Twain, and Henry James. 105 rooms.

Locarno *(near Piazza del Popolo)* ✪✪ *Via della Penna 22, 00186; Tel. 3610841/3216030; fax 3215249.* Centrally located hotel with a charming vine-covered façade. 38 comfortable rooms.

Lord Byron ✪✪✪ *Via Giuseppe De Notaris 5, 00197; Tel. 3220404; fax 3220405.* Elegant hotel hosting one of Rome's most distinguished restaurants, Relais le Jardin. Garden. 37 rooms.

Rome

Majestic ✪✪✪ *Via V. Veneto 50, 00187; Tel. 486841; fax 4880984.* Tastefully refurbished in deluxe style, this hotel is a perfect blend of old and new. Every room is individually furnished and all bathrooms are complete with white Carrara marble and Jacuzzi bathtubs. 94 rooms.

Margutta *(Piazza del Popolo/Corso)* ✪ *Via Laurina 34, 00187; Tel. 3223674; fax 32200395.* Small but centrally located hotel. Some of the rooms on the upper floor have their own terraces. 21 rooms.

Mediterraneo *(near Termini Station)* ✪✪✪ *Via Cavour 15, 00184; Tel. 4884051; fax 4744105.* A period piece from the 1930s in solemn Classical style, with busts and statues, mosaics, and maps all on the theme of the Mediterranean. Wonderful views over the city from the terrace on the tenth floor. 262 rooms.

Milani *(near Termini Station)* ✪✪ *Via Magenta 12, 00185; Tel. 4457051; fax 4462317.* On the more sedate side of Termini Station. Efficient service. 78 rooms.

Portoghesi *(near Piazza Navona)* ✪ *Via dei Portoghesi 1, 00186; Tel. 6864231; fax 6876976.* Comfortable, small hotel in a quiet corner of Rome's Centro Storico. Reasonably priced with air conditioning, television, and telephones in each of the 27 rooms.

Quirinale *(near Piazza della Repubblica)* ✪✪✪ *Via Nazionale 7, 00184; Tel. 4707; fax 4820099.* Large hotel just next door to the charming Teatro dell'Opera. Garden. Outdoor dining in summer. 201 rooms.

Raphael *(near Piazza Navona)* ✪✪✪ *Largo Febo 2, 00186; Tel. 682831; fax 6878993.* Vine-covered and intimate establishment, decorated with antiques in the lobby as well as the rooms. There is both a restaurant and bar in the hotel. 83 rooms.

Sant'Anselmo *(Aventine)* ✪✪ *Piazza Sant'Anselmo 2, 00153; Tel. 574819; fax 5783604*. Very peaceful hotel with a pretty garden on the Aventine but not all that convenient if you want to spend most of your time in the centre of the city. 45 rooms.

Scalinata di Spagna *(above Piazza di Spagna)* ✪✪ *Piazza Trinità dei Monti 17, 00187; Tel. 6793006; fax 6840598*. You will have a fantastic view over the city and down the Spanish Steps from this charming small establishment. No restaurant. 15 rooms.

Senato *(near the Pantheon)* ✪ *Piazza della Rotonda 73, 00186; Tel. 6793231; fax 69940297*. Comfortable hotel in the heart of Rome's historical centre. Some of the 51 rooms have a view of the Pantheon.

Sole *(near Campo dei Fiori)* ✪ *Via del Biscione 76, 00186; Tel. 6879446/6879446; fax 6893787*. Budget-priced hotel in a convenient location. 58 rooms.

Sole Al Pantheon *(near the Pantheon)* ✪✪✪ *Piazza della Rotonda 63, 00186; Tel. 6780441; fax 69940689*. An inn for 500 years, the hotel has recently been refurbished, retaining all its charm while adding modern comforts. Each of the 25 rooms is named after one of the illustrious guests of the past.

Suisse *(near Piazza di Spagna)* ✪ *Via Gregoriana 56, 00187; Tel. 6783649; fax 6781258*. Comfortable, efficiently-run hotel in a good location near the Spanish Steps. 28 rooms.

Villa Delle Rose *(near Termini Station)* ✪ *Via Vicenza 5, 00185; Tel. 4451788; fax 4451639*. A former villa with a frescoed salon for a lounge, and a garden. Efficient and attractive. 37 rooms.

Recommended Restaurants

Authentic Roman cuisine has its basis in *la cucina povera,* the cooking of the poor. You will therefore find simple but delicious traditional dishes in many a Roman *trattoria,* but also in the most elegant and expensive of restaurants. Below is a list of restaurants recommended by Berlitz; if you find other places worth recommending we'd be pleased to hear from you.

Note that after the *Ferragosto* festival (15 August) many restaurants close for two weeks as Romans head out of town.

The following symbols are designed to give you some idea of the price for a three-course meal with wine:

✪	below L 40,000
✪✪	L 40,000-70,000
✪✪✪	above L 70,000

Agustarello a Testaccio *(Testaccio)* ✪ *Via G. Branca 98/100; Tel. 5746585.* Typical family-run *trattoria* with authentic Roman cooking. Good house wine from the Roman hills. Definitely not for the calorie-conscious. Closed Sunday and from 15 August to 15 September.

Alberto Ciarla *(Trastevere)* ✪✪✪ *Piazza San Cosimato 40, 00153; Tel. (06) 5818668.* The city's top restaurant for seafood and fish dishes, and worth a visit for the fish tank alone. Outdoor dining is available; note that the restaurant is closed at lunchtime. Advance booking is advised. Closed Sunday and from January 12 – 19 and August 10 – 20.

Andrea *(near Via Veneto)* ✪✪✪ *Via Sardegna 26, 00187; Tel. 4821891.* Classic Italian cuisine in a classy setting. The best hors d'œuvres in Rome are to be found here as well as excellent seafood dishes. Good wine list. Reservations are recommended. Closed Sunday, Monday lunchtime, and during most of August.

Apuleius *(Aventine)* ✪✪ *Via Tempio di Diana 15, 00153; Tel. 5742160/5746509; fax 5746509.* Quiet restaurant in a first-century Roman house serving seafood and hearty fare. A good midday stopping point for Aventine sightseers. Closed Sunday.

Il Buco *(Corso/Pantheon)* ✪✪ *Via di Sant'Ignazio 8, 00186; Tel. 6793298/6784467.* Popular *trattoria* serving Tuscan specialities, with some dishes from Lazio as well. Closed Monday and 2 weeks in August.

Campana *(near Piazza Navona)* ✪✪ *Vicolo della Campana 18, 00186; Tel. 6867820.* A popular local *trattoria* with all Italian favourites on the menu. Closed Monday and for the month of August.

Camponeschi *(Campo dei Fiori/Via Giulia)* ✪✪ *Piazza Farnese 50, 00186; Tel. 6874927.* Sophisticated menu and an elegant dining room with terrace view. Reservations advised. Open until late. Closed Sunday and for two weeks in August.

Cannavota *(St. John Lateran)* ✪✪ *Piazza di San Giovanni in Laterano 20, 00184; Tel. 77205007.* Charming, easy-going *trattoria* and one of the more popular haunts in the capital, offering big portions. Especially good for lasagna, risotto, and grilled fish. Closed Wednesday and for three weeks in August.

Casina Valadier *(above Piazza del Popolo)* ✪✪ *Viale Belvedere al Pincio; Tel. 6792083.* A romantic location in the park of the Villa Borghese, with one of Rome's most splendid views, dominated by the great dome of St. Peter's. Cuisine based on Italian regional cooking. Romans come here more for the atmosphere than the food. Reservations essential in the evening and at weekends. Closed Monday.

Cecilia Metella *(Old Appian Way)* ✪✪ *Via Appia Antica 125/127, 00179; Tel. 5136743.* Pleasant, with shady garden, near the Roman tomb of Cecilia Metella. Closed Monday and several weeks in August.

Checchino dal 1887 *(Testaccio)* ✪✪ *Via Monte Testaccio 30, 00153; Tel. 5743816.* A former *trattoria* serving a cuisine based on the cheap cuts and offal from Testaccio's slaughterhouse. Tripe, brains, liver, sweetbreads, and intestines are still the starting ingredients. Reserve for supper. Closed Sunday, Monday, in August, and over Christmas.

Checco er Carrettiere *(Trastevere)* ✪✪ *Via Benedetta 10, 00153; Tel. 5817018.* Colourful Trastevere tavern. Outdoor tables in summer. Booking advised. Closed Sunday evening, Monday and 10 August to 10 September.

Al Chianti *(Porta Pia)* ✪✪ *Via Ancona 17, 00198; Tel. 44291534.* Tuscan cooking. Reservations advised. Closed Sunday; for several weeks in August.

Colline Emiliane *(near Piazza Barberini)* ✪✪ *Via degli Avignonesi 22, 00187; Tel. 4817538.* Trattoria serving specialities from Emilia-Romagna. Advance bookings advised. Closed Friday and during August.

Corallo *(Piazza Navona)* ✪ *Via del Corallo 10; Tel. 68307703.* Good pizzas and speciality cooking. The parma ham and *focaccia* (plain pizza) are particularly recommended.

Coriolano *(near Porta Pia)* ✪✪✪ *Via Ancona 14, 00198; Tel. 44249863.* An elegant place serving very nicely presented versions of hearty Roman fare and home-made pasta dishes. Reservations advised. Closed Sunday, weekends in July, and most of August.

Il Cortiletto *(near Pantheon)* ✪✪ *Piazza Capranica 77, 00186; Tel. 6793977.* Charming restaurant offering traditional dishes such as risotto, *carpaccio,* and many rich desserts. Closed Tuesday.

Crisciotti-al Boschetto (*near Via Nazionale*) ✪ *Via del Boschetto 30, 00184; Tel. 4744770*. Rustic *trattoria* with delightful outdoor dining. Closed Saturday and August.

Il Drappo (*Corso Vittorio Emanuele/Via Giulia*) ✪✪ *Vicolo del Malpasso 9, 00186; Tel. 6877365*. Small and attractive restaurant serving classic Sardinian dishes and wines. Reserve. Closed Sunday and during August.

L'Eau Vive (*near Largo Argentina*) ✪✪ *Via Monterone 85, 00186; Tel. 68801095*. Splendid French-Colonial cuisine served in a restaurant run by French nuns and housed in a 16th-century papal palace. Advance reservations advised. Closed on Sunday and August.

Il Giardino (*near Piazza Barberini*) ✪✪ *Via Zucchelli 29; Tel. 465202*. Delicious Roman cuisine. Very good value for money. Try the *assaini della cas*.

Giovanni (*near Via Veneto*) ✪✪ *Via Marche 19; Tel. 4821834*. Popular local restaurant serving good pasta dishes. Advance reservations are advised. Closed Friday evening, all day Saturday, and for the month of August.

Al Girarrosto Da Ezio ✪✪ *Via Germanico, 56; Tel. 39725717*. Well-situated restaurant near St. Peter's. The principal specialities are Tuscan and Roman dishes. Particularly recommended for meat lovers. Closed Monday and for three weeks in August.

Hassler Roof Garden (*above Piazza di Spagna*) ✪✪✪ *Piazza della Trinità dei Monti 6, 00187; Tel. 6792651*. A restaurant at the top of the Hassler Hotel with a romantic view of the whole city. Excellent service and food. Advance reservations are advised.

Insalata Ricca I (*near Corso Vittorio Emanuele*) ✪ *Largo dei Chiavari, 85; Tel. 68803656*. Nice variety of fresh and savoury salads as well as succulent pasta dishes. No smoking. Closed Wednesday.

Margutta Vegetariano *(near Piazza del Popolo)* ✪✪ *Via Margutta 119; Tel. 6786033.* Traditional vegetarian dishes from southern Italy served in pretty surroundings. Closed Sunday.

Mariano *(near Via Veneto)* ✪✪ *Via Piemonte 79; 00187. Tel. 4745256.* Regional cheeses and home-style cooking from the Marches. Reservation advised. Closed Saturday lunchtime, Sunday, and August.

Il Matriciano *(Prati)* ✪✪ *Via dei Gracchi 55, 00192; Tel. 3212327.* Situated close to the Vatican. Roman specialities served in a very comfortable atmosphere. Advance reservations are advised. Closed on Wednesday from October to mid-June and on Saturday throughout the remainder of the year. Also closed for the month of August.

Al Moro *(near Trevi Fountain)* ✪✪ *Vicolo delle Bollette 13, between Via dei Crociferi and Via delle Muratte; Tel. 6783495.* Busy, crowded place with excellent versions of salt cod and vegetable dishes. Reservation advised. Closed Sunday and for the month of August.

Nel Regno di Re Ferdinando *(near Piazza Navona)* ✪✪ *Via dei Banchi Nuovi 8, 00186; Tel. 68801167.* Wonderful Neapolitan pasta dishes, seafood, and pastries. Open evenings only. Late-night dining. Closed Sunday and for two weeks in August.

Nino *(Corso/Piazza di Spagna)* ✪✪ *Via Borgogna 11; Tel. 6795676.* Good traditional Tuscan food and wine. Try the Tuscan-style beans. Closed Sunday and in August.

L'Orso 80 *(near Piazza Navona)* ✪✪ *Via dell'Orso 33, 00186; Tel. 6864904/6861710.* Uncomplicated meat and fish dishes cooked in the style of the Abruzzo. A friendly family-run restaurant. Closed Monday and for several weeks in August.

Der Pallaro (*Corso Vittoria Emanuele*) ✪ *Largo del Pallaro; Tel. 68801488*. Authentic family-run Roman *trattoria*. Friendly atmosphere. Set menus changed every day right from hors d'œuvres down to dessert. To conclude the evening, try some of owner Mario's mandarin liqueur. Closed Monday and in August.

Papà Giovanni (*near Piazza Navona*) ✪✪✪ *Via dei Sediari 4; Tel. 68804807*. One of the city's top restaurants, where simple and classical dishes are prepared with style. The accent is on seasonal vegetables and fresh Lazio market produce. In addition there is good list of local wines. Closed Sunday.

Paris in Trastevere (*Trastevere*) ✪✪ *Piazza di San Callisto 7/a, 00153; Tel. 5815378*. On offer at this delightful restaurant are a charming Baroque dining room and a terrace for summer suppers. Closed Sunday evening, all day Monday and in August.

La Pergola dell' Hotel Hilton (*Monte Mario*) ✪✪✪ *Via Cadlolo 101, 00136; Tel. 35091*. Elegant penthouse restaurant with spectacular view overlooking the city and Roman hills. Reservations essential. Closed Sunday.

Piccola Roma Da Ezio (*Montecitorio/Corso*) ✪✪✪ *Via Uffici del Vicario 36, 00186; Tel. 6798606*. Good food in beautiful setting on the first floor of an old Roman palace. Closed Sunday and during August.

Al Piccolo Arancio (*near Trevi Fountain*) ✪ *Vicolo di Scanderberg 112; Tel. 6786139*. In a narrow alley near the Trevi Fountain, this is an attractive little place which takes food seriously. Very good Roman specialities and fish. Closed Monday and for the month of August.

Il Piccolo (*near Piazza Navona*) ✪ *Via del Governo Vecchio 74; Tel. 68801746*. Lively and central wine bar with a buffet serving traditional fare. Closed Tuesday; evenings only Saturday and Sunday.

Piperno *(Ghetto)* ✪✪✪ *Via Monte dei Cenci 9, 00186; Tel. 6542772.* Expensive restaurant in the heart of the ghetto serving Roman/Jewish specialities. Reservations advised. Closed Sunday evening and Monday.

Pizzeria Baffetto *(near Piazza Navona)* ✪ *Via del Governo Vecchio 114; Tel. 6861617.* A student hangout. The pizza is excellent. Closed Monday.

Pizzeria MonteCarlo *(near Corso Vittorio Emanuele)* ✪ *Vicolo Savelli, 11/A - 13, 00186; Tel. 6861877.* Excellent pizza. Student hangout.

Pizzeria Panattoni *(Trastevere)* ✪ *Viale de Trastevere 53; Tel. 5800919.* Very popular. Good pizza and other Roman specialities.

Al Pompiere *(near Largo Argentina)* ✪✪ *Via di Santa Maria dei Calderai 38; Tel. 6868377.* Traditional Roman cooking prepared and served with great finesse in the heart of a busy quarter. Closed Sunday and mid-July to late August.

Relais la Piscine *(Parioli)* ✪✪✪ *Via G Mangili 6, 00197; Tel. 3216126.* Creative cuisine with some Mediterranean and French inspiration and ingredients. Reservations advised. Closed Sunday evening.

Relais le Jardin *(Parioli)* ✪✪✪ *Via Giuseppe De Notaris 5; Tel. 3220404.* Listed among the top ten restaurants in Italy, this is probably the finest restaurant in Rome. Excellent cuisine in the elegant atmosphere of the Hotel Lord Byron (see page 133). Reservations essential. Closed Sunday and for most of the month of August.

Le Restaurant del Grand Hotel *(near Termini Station)* ✪✪✪ *Via V.E. Orlando 3; Tel. 4709.* Sophisticated cuisine in the setting of the splendidly luxurious dining rooms of the Grand Hotel. Reservations essential.

Romolo a Porta Settimiana *(Trastevere)* ✪✪ *Via di Porta Settimiana 8; Tel. 5818284.* Classical Roman and also some very creative pasta dishes. Outdoor dining in the terraced garden in summer. Open late. Reservations advised. Closed Monday and for most of the month of August.

La Rosetta *(Corso/Piazza Navona)* ✪✪✪ *Via della Rosetta 9; Tel. 68308841.* Excellent seafood restaurant near the Pantheon. Reservations essential. Closed Sunday and during August.

Sans Souci *(near Via Veneto)* ✪✪✪✪ *Via Sicilia 20; Tel. 4821814.* Elegant restaurant offering a good range of international cuisine and traditional Roman dishes. Dinner only. Late-night suppers available. Reservations are advised. Closed on Mondays and for three weeks in August.

Taverna Flavia *(near Via XX Settembre)* ✪✪ *Via Flavia 9; Tel. 4745214.* Fashionable taverna open late. Closed for Saturday lunch and all day Sunday.

Taverna Giulia *(Corso Vittorio Emanuele/Tiber)* ✪✪ *Vicolo dell'Oro 23; Tel. 6869768.* Ligurian cuisine, much of it green, the most famous of the dishes being *pesto* (basil sauce). Reservations are essential. Closed on Sundays and in August.

Taverna Trevi *(Fontana di Trevi)* ✪✪ *Via del Lavatore, 82; Tel. 6792470.* An extensive menu offers many local specialities, and service is good. A range of dishes available according to budget.

El Toulà *(Corso/Piazza Navona)* ✪✪✪ *Via della Lupa 29/b; Tel. 6873498/6873750.* Elegant, popular restaurant near Piazza del Parliamento. Notable wine list. Reservations essential. Closed Saturday at lunch, all day Sunday and in August.

Trimani Wine Bar *(Piazza della Repubblica)* ✪ *Via Cernaia 37/b; Tel. 446930.* Excellent choice of wines and good food in elegant and friendly atmosphere. You can have a glass of wine or a full meal at very reasonable prices. Closed all day on Sunday.

Vecchia Roma *(near Piazza Venezia)* ✪✪ *Piazza di Campitelli 18; Tel. 6864604.* A lovely spot offering tables on the square in the summer and cosy dining rooms in the winter. A long list of dishes based on traditional, local ingredients. Reservations advised. Closed Wednesday and for 15 days in August.

LAZIO

Adriano ✪✪ *Via Villa Adriano, Tivoli; Tel. (0774) 382235.* Stop for a plate of delicious home-made pasta and a glass of wine after a walk round Hadrian's villa. Pleasant open-air dining in the summer. Closed Sunday evening.

Allo Sbarco di Enea ✪✪ *Via dei Romagnoli 675, 00119 Ostia Antica; Tel. (06) 5650034.* Mock-ancient frescoes, chariots, and waiters decked out in Roman costumes. Between the station and the ruins. Closed Monday.

Bastianelli al Moro ✪✪✪ *Via Torre Clementina 312, 00054 Fiumicino; Tel. (06) 6505358.* Excellent restaurant specializing in seafood. Closed Monday and for most of the month of January.

Cacciani ✪✪ *Via Diaz 13, 00044 Frascati; Tel. (06) 9420378.* Good cuisine, with outdoor dining in summer. Closed on Sunday evenings from November to March, on Tuesdays, and during the last two weeks of August.